THE PERFECT HORSE

THE PERFECT HORSE

The Daring Rescue of
Horses Kidnapped
by Hitler

Adapted for Young People

ELIZABETH LETTS

DELACORTE PRESS

Photo credits located on page 243.

Visit us on the Web! rhcbooks.com

Educators and librarians, for a variety of teaching tools, visit us at
RHTeachersLibrarians.com

Library of Congress Cataloging-in-Publication Data
Name: Letts, Elizabeth, author.
Title: The perfect horse : The Daring Rescue of Horses Kidnapped by Hitler /Elizabeth
Letts.
Description: First edition. | New York : Delacorte Press, [2019] | "Adapted for young people."
| "Originally published in hardcover in the United States by Ballantine Books, an imprint of
Random House, a division of Penguin Random House LLC, New York in 2016." | Summary:
American soldiers, aided by an Austrian colonel who was both an Olympiar and a trainer of
Lipizzaners, attempt to kidnap horses that had been taken by Nazis "for the glorification of
the Third Reich" and smuggle them to safety.
Identifiers: LCCN 2017060606 | ISBN 978-0-525-64474-3 (hc) |
ISBN 978-0-525-64476-7 (glb) | ISBN 978-0-525-64475-0 (el)
Subjects: LCSH: World War, 1939–1945—Juvenile fiction. | CYAC: World War,
1939–1945—Fiction. | Lipizzaner horse—Fiction. | Arabian horse—Fiction. | Horses—
Fiction. | Podhajsky, Alois—Fiction. | United States. Army—History—World War,
1939–1945—Fiction.
Classification: LCC PZ7.1.L4853 Per 2019 | DDC [Fic]—dc23

The text of this book is set in 12-point Adobe Jenson.
Interior design by Trish Parcell

This book is dedicated to my family members who served:

W. Jackson Letts, second lieutenant, U.S. Army, Korea

And to the memory of

J. Spencer Letts, *reserve captain, U.S. Army*
Vern Carroll, *captain, U.S. Marine Corps*, Korea
Verny Carroll, *commander, U.S. Navy*, World War I and World War II

To the men of the 2nd Calvary and their families

And to all the fallen horses—may we honor their sacrifice

Courage is being scared to death . . .
and saddling up anyway.
—John Wayne

CONTENTS

LIST OF CHARACTERS

THE EUROPEANS

Andrzej Kristalovich (Andrzej Krzysztalowicz): /Ahn-JAY Kshee-STAL-o-veech/ Director of Poland's national stud farm.

Rudolf Lessing: German army veterinarian stationed at the Hostau stud farm in Czechoslovakia.

Alois Podhajsky: /AH-loys Pod-HEY-skee/ Austrian director of the Spanish Riding School of Vienna.

Gustav Rau: German horse expert. Chief equerry in charge of all horse breeding in the Third Reich.

Hubert Rudofsky: Czech-born ethnic German. Director of the stud farm in Hostau, Czechoslovakia.

Jan Ziniewicz: /Yahn ZEE-nee-ev-eech/ Chief groom of Poland's National Stud Farm.

THE AMERICANS

Lieutenant William Donald "Quin" Quinlivan: Career cavalryman. Assigned to the 42nd Squadron of the 2nd Cavalry.

Colonel Charles Hancock "Hank" Reed: Virginia-born, expert horseman, commanding officer of the 2nd Cavalry.

Captain Ferdinand Sperl: Swiss-born naturalized U.S. citizen. Interrogator attached to the 2nd Cavalry.

Captain Thomas Stewart: Son of a Tennessee senator. Intelligence officer in the 2nd Cavalry.

THE HORSES

Neapolitano Africa: Austrian Lipizzaner performing stallion, one of Alois Podhajsky's personal mounts.

Pluto Theodorosta: Austrian Lipizzaner performing stallion, one of Alois Podhajsky's personal mounts.

Witez: /VEE-tezh/ Bay Arabian stallion foaled in Poland in 1938. His official registered name was Witez II.

PROLOGUE

BOMBARDMENT

Vienna, Austria, September 10, 1944

A shrill air raid signal pierced the quiet of the cobblestoned Michaelerplatz, a plaza in the heart of Vienna, Austria. Tucked away from view, in the elegant horse stables of the Hofburg Palace, thirty-three majestic white stallions startled, pawing and rearing, their eyes full of fear. The city was under siege.

Peering out of a box stall, one eight-year-old Lipizzaner horse stood perfectly still, his white coat glowing in the stable's dim light. His ears pricked forward as he listened for his master's footsteps through the din of airplanes roaring overhead. Next to his stall, on a small black slate, his name, Neapolitano Africa, and his birthdate, 1935, were neatly stenciled in white paint.

A slim middle-aged gentleman rushed to Africa's side, whispering a word of reassurance, then placing a warm hand on the stallion's shoulder. Alois Podhajsky was utterly concentrated on a single goal—to keep his stallions safe. Carefully, Podhajsky slipped a polished leather halter from its peg next to the stall.

The stallion lowered his head and placed his muzzle through the leather noseband, helping to make the task easier. His eyes seemed to say, "I know what's going on here. Let me help."

By now the entire stable was a hive of activity: stableboys, also known as *grooms*, quickly haltered some of the stallions, while riders, in their buckskin britches and jackets, took charge of others.

In single file, the horses and men crossed a large courtyard and clattered through a deserted city street until they reached a sheltered hallway. The stallions had calmed down, even as the loud booms and crashes almost drowned out the ringing of their iron shoes on the cobblestones. The last to enter the shelter of the hallway was Alois Podhajsky, Olympic equestrian and director of the Spanish Riding School of Vienna. The enormous wooden doors swung shut behind them; here, the thick walls muffled the sounds a bit. For the first moment since hearing the air raid signal, Podhajsky took a deep breath. He reached into the leather pouch at his hip, extracted a sugar lump, and offered it to Africa, feeling the tickle of the horse's whiskers as he nibbled it from Podhajsky's bare palm. Horse and man were clearly intimate and seemed to converse without words, providing each other silent reassurance.

The Spanish Riding School of Vienna was one of Austria's most beloved institutions. Named because the original horses came from Spain, the school famously showcased one of the world's finest and rarest breeds: the royal Lipizzaners. With their snow-white coats, their large aristocratic heads, and their deep brown eyes, these horses were unlike any others in the world.

Around them, war raged in all directions. These royal

horses had escaped danger many times. They had fled for their lives from Napoleon's armies, and again during World War I. But now, in the all-out war of air and ground that was engulfing Europe, where could they go? No obvious path to safety lay before them.

A loud boom ripped through the building. Next came a deafening thud; glass shattered high above them. A cacophony of neighs tore through the dust-choked air. Podhajsky and Africa turned to look at each other. Podhajsky gripped the sturdy lead rope, held his breath, and waited.

PART ONE

The Europeans

1.

AN UNLIKELY OLYMPIAN

Berlin, Germany, 1936

Alois Podhajsky looked as if he'd been born to sit astride a horse. His long, straight torso had no awkward angles, no rounded curves, nothing to distract from its elegant lines. But to look at the Austrian officer's somber expression was to understand that within, he carried a shadow. In 1918, after being severely wounded while serving in World War I, he had suffered from shell shock. If anything had brought him back to life, it was his love for horses.

On June 12, 1936, Alois Podhajsky straddled his mount, Nero, ready to enter the May Field, the site of the Olympic competition in equestrian dressage. Descended from intricate military maneuvers developed in ancient times, dressage asks horse and rider to perform a series of carefully outlined movements. Just as ballroom dancing and pair skating command partners to work together seamlessly, in the sport of dressage, the rider completes an intricate dance with his partner— a twelve-hundred-pound four-footed beast. Great dressage demands the ability to communicate with a mount in the silent language of horsemanship.

The fact that this pair was competing here, in the eleventh Olympic Games, against the top equestrian contenders from around the world, was unlikely indeed. Nero, a gangly brown Thoroughbred, had been bred to race, but having proven slow, he had been cast off for use as an army cavalry mount. The gelding had shown equally little talent as a soldier's charger, and the army had nearly sold him off before Podhajsky decided that the horse showed potential and saved him from the auction block. Podhajsky too was an almost-reject. He had been kicked out of Austria's prestigious cavalry officer training school after an injury. He would never forget the day in 1928 when his riding instructor said, "You're finished." But Podhajsky had pressed on, wholeheartedly committed to the art of dressage, until even the finest equestrian experts could no longer ignore his skill.

Just three years later, Podhajsky received the Austrian cavalry's highest honor: In 1931, he was sent to study at the world's oldest academy of classical riding, the Spanish Riding School. Podhajsky's love for horses, for riding, for life, had been restored. Now, five years after being expelled from the cavalry school, he was representing his country at the Olympics. While Nero was neither flashy nor handsome, he was eager and co-operative. With several years of training, the two had risen to the top of the sport.

Podhajsky's own love of Austria's equestrian traditions had started during his childhood, and at eighteen, he'd joined the cavalry. The ornate uniform—fur-muffed, spike-helmeted, brass-buttoned—made him look like a boy playing dress-up in his father's clothes. But Austria lost both the Great War and its empire. The traditions to which he had sworn boyhood allegiance were mostly gone. What remained of the great Austrian empire was its tradition of horsemanship, which Podhajsky still believed was the best in the world. Now was his chance to prove it.

Nero's form was impeccable. Podhajsky looked dazzling in the olive uniform of the Austrian Republic. The failed racehorse and his reject rider were preparing to compete in one of the most difficult equestrian sports. Podhajsky had committed to memory the complex series of movements that he would need to execute perfectly. Timing and placement were everything. If his horse stepped out of the barriers that marked the boundaries of the ring, he would be eliminated.

In the sport of dressage, the rider spends years teaching a horse to perform movements on command. The horse has four ordinary paces: walk, trot, canter, and gallop, each with a different cadence. In an advanced dressage test, a rider may ask a horse to perform a *pirouette*, a move in which the horse's hindquarters remain almost in place while his forelegs canter a full circle around them. Movements like this had been taught slowly, in a step-by-step process that took years to complete.

As he awaited his turn, Podhajsky hoped that his own long years of practice would pay off. In a chaotic postwar world, he wanted to embody what his patient training stood for— discipline, tradition, passion, and perfection for its own sake. Winning a medal might be the final outcome of this endeavor, but for Podhajsky, the endeavor itself mattered most.

Riders from twenty-one countries had gathered to compete in the equestrian events at the summer '36 Games. Podhajsky knew that his stiffest competition came from the Germans, who had a home field advantage. He lifted his eyes to look at the spectators. The arena's clipped lawn was laid out with geometrical precision. In the distance, the impressive hulk of Olympia Stadium filled the horizon, festooned with the flags of many nations. Evenly spaced scarlet Nazi swastika banners stained its perimeter.

As he looked across the field at the international panel of judges assembled there, he knew that this was more than just a competition. Three years earlier, Hitler had catapulted into power. He was determined that the Berlin Olympics would showcase the Nazi Party's Aryan ideals, and perhaps even prove their superiority. Hitler was using the Olympics as a piece of nationalistic, pro-Nazi theater. The Nazis, in a clever propaganda move, had camouflaged many of the blatant anti-Jewish policies that were already being enforced in Berlin, removing anti-Semitic signs and removing harsh propaganda from newspapers, but the menace and violence lurked just beneath the whitewashed surface.

At one end of the judges' platform, his face in a concentrated scowl, sat the most influential person at the equestrian site, Gustav Rau. Clad in a dark suit, his bald head covered by a felt fedora, this fifty-six-year-old German was the mastermind behind the Olympian equestrian events, including the selection of the judges.

Gustav Rau recognized the next competitor who entered the ring. Alois Podhajsky was the winner of several important competitions leading up to the Olympics, beating out top German entries.

Podhajsky's movements were barely perceptible as he short-ened his reins, a signal to Nero that they were soon to begin. He relaxed his thighs and sank deeper into his saddle; he turned inward, listening to his mount. An old adage says that a good rider can hear his horse speak and a great rider can hear his horse whisper. As Podhajsky listened to Nero's whisper, the whole world fell away, the flags, the crowds, even his own wish to win. All that was left was himself, his horse, and the signal that passed between them, like a radio tuned to a frequency that only the two of them could hear.

When the ringmaster gave the signal, Podhajsky and Nero entered on a straight line at a controlled gallop, stopping on a dime precisely in the center of the arena. Nero stood as still as a statue while Podhajsky swept off his military cap to salute the judges. Then the pair continued at a free walk, a deceptively simple movement that tested a horse's perfect obedience. With no visible cue from his rider, Nero picked up a floating trot and proceeded to zigzag through the arena, flawlessly executing each complex movement. The horse looked bright and lively, while his rider remained serenely motionless. The crowd leaned forward in their seats.

As Podhajsky turned back down the center line of the arena, the world seemed to glow in vivid hues. His ride had gone flaw-lessly. Well-wishers crowded around him, assuring him that he was certain to take home the gold medal. Calmly, he extracted a sugar lump from his pocket, and the adoring crowd watched quietly while Nero daintily nuzzled up the treat from the palm of his master's outstretched hand.

Meanwhile, seated on the platform, the German judge was adding up his marks. Realizing that the Austrian had the best score, he stealthily erased a few marks on his scorecard. Then he penciled in a lower mark.

The following day, on June 13, 1936, Alois Podhajsky stood on the podium. He and Nero had finished in third place. In the end, Germany gained all of the gold medals. Later, when Gustav Rau penned the official review of the Olympic equestrian events, he claimed that only German superiority—not any favoritism—had led to the medal count.

Though he hadn't made first place, Podhajsky returned to Austria a national hero. He was a representative of a young democracy, the Republic of Austria, and had demonstrated one of Austria's greatest prides, its equestrian prowess, in front of the world.

Neither of these men knew that their paths would cross again. Each man would have a mission: Alois Podhajsky would soon be entrusted with safeguarding one of his nation's most important cultural treasures. Gustav Rau would be determined to seize those treasures for Nazi Germany.

2.

THE MASTER OF ALL HORSES

On May 8, 1938, two months after Hitler's Reich conquered Austria, Gustav Rau docked at New York Harbor on the German luxury liner *Bremen*. Accompanying Rau was his wife, Helga, herself an accomplished horsewoman, along with some of Germany's most prominent horse lovers, for an equestrian sightseeing tour of America.

Ever since his triumph in Berlin in '36, Gustav Rau had received a new high-powered title: chief equerry of Germany and master of the horse. And he had developed an obsession: horse breeding.

Breeding horses for specific purposes had been practiced in Europe for hundreds of years. Human and equine life were deeply intertwined, since people's businesses and lives depended on equestrian help for almost every task—from transportation to heavy lifting to warfare. Each kind of horse was bred for certain skills. For example, riding horses need speed and good temperaments. Plow horses need brute strength. And military

horses are best if they have hearty constitutions and don't require much food. Breeders had managed to tweak or modify
their equestrian companions through trial and error—but the
science behind these changes remained poorly understood.

In German, the word *Rasse* means both "race" of people and
"breed" of animal. Sinisterly, Rau's theories reflected this double meaning. He believed horses should be bred to be identical,
and similarly, he believed people should have "unmixed" blood,
and be mated for their racial "purity."

The Nazis became interested in Gustav Rau's theories
about pure-blooded horses, believing that the same laws could
be applied to human beings. The Nazis had developed a theory
known as *Blut und Boden*, or blood and land—which claimed
that German rural people were "pure-blooded" and therefore
better than other people. The Nazis believed that these so-
called pure-blooded people deserved to have more room to grow
and expand, a policy called *Lebensraum* (living space). This idea
motivated Nazis to seize land from other countries. The people
who already lived in those countries would be either forced to
work in German factories or moved into concentration camps.

By May 1938, when Rau and his party arrived in New
York, events in Nazi Germany were taking an ominous turn. In
March, Germany indeed captured more land when it invaded
Austria. In a mere six months, the persecution of the Jews
would reach terrifying heights. Rau would be unfazed by these
horrors, even when crazed mobs would storm the streets of
Berlin and other large cities, burning synagogues and smashing
Jewish-owned store windows during Kristallnacht, the night of
broken glass.

In fact, Rau was pleased that the Nazis shared his enthusiasm. He seemed only too happy to impress these powerful allies. The English were renowned for their Thoroughbreds; Poland bred the world's finest Arabian horses; and soon, Rau plotted, the German nation would produce the greatest military horse.

The first stop on the Reich equestrians' American tour was Elmont, New York, for a visit to the iconic Gilded Age racetrack Belmont Park. Rau and his guests were eager to see American Thoroughbred horse racing on display. American horses are descended from heavier English draft horses bred with Middle Eastern stallions back in the seventeeth and eighteenth centuries, producing a lighter, faster horse that proved adept at racing. By the middle of the nineteenth century, selective breeding had created a bigger, speedier horse.

In many ways, the trial-and-error successes of horse breeding had surpassed the state of the science. Before the discovery of DNA, scientists did not know exactly *how* traits were transmitted from parent to offspring. The refinement of the Thoroughbred horse had demonstrated that by choosing carefully which horses to breed, they could influence basic qualities (such as size and color), and they believed that perhaps more complex qualities (like heart and temperament) could be inherited when certain horses were mated.

As Rau admired Belmont Park's Thoroughbreds, a field of "science" called eugenics was very much on his mind. Now discredited, eugenics explored the notion that mankind could be improved by using principles similar to those that had created the Thoroughbred. It was believed that human pedigrees could be created just like the kind that already existed for horses, with the aim of identifying both "strong" bloodlines and "weak" ones. Since then, scientists have learned that breeding does not determine complex qualities such as intelligence, courage, and behavior.

Sir Francis Galton, a cousin of Charles Darwin, first coined the term *eugenics* in his 1883 book *Human Faculty and Its Development*. Eugenicists believed that just as horse breeders could breed a bigger, swifter, better racehorse, scientists could eventually eliminate from the human population those considered "undesirables"—which could run the gamut from people who were severely developmentally delayed to people who were alcoholic or unemployed. Galton and his followers imagined a future in which society had become homogenized and social ills had been, quite sinisterly, bred out of the population.

The Reich visitors were already familiar with the concept of a "human pedigree." In order to be accepted as a member of the Nazi Party, an individual needed to be able to demonstrate that he or she had "pure blood" that went back at least four generations. Party members were also required to carry a document to prove their Aryan ancestry.

After Belmont Park and a day of sightseeing in Manhattan, the German equestrians' next stop on the tour was a visit north to Goshen, New York, to see a famous stable of American trotting horses bred by E. Roland Harriman. Here, the Reich equestrians would have the opportunity to see modern breeding at its most refined level. Rau paid close attention to their tour guide.

The American Standardbred differs in important ways from

his more storied racing brother, the Thoroughbred. The Standardbred is judged not by his noble ancestry but by his ability
to perform a specific task: to trot the distance of one mile in
less than two minutes and thirty seconds. Thoroughbreds are
all descended from three specific stallions that lived in England
in the eighteenth century, so they are like members of a royal
family, all related by blood. But the American Standardbred is
not the same. Originally, any horse with the right size, temperament, or skill could be bred as a Standardbred. The breeder's
goal was to breed a horse that was a good, strong, fast trotter.
This practice would have been of much interest to Rau, whose
dream was to create a breed of German military horses that
would be as closely matched as industrially produced machines.

Soon, Rau's group reached their final destination: Fort
Leavenworth, Kansas, one of the U.S. Army's impressive western cavalry schools, where Rau could see their breeding program firsthand. The Americans had started their program in
1918. Unlike Rau, they didn't seek "pure-bloodedness"; rather,
they sought out stallions with desirable characteristics such as
hardiness, good temperament, soundness, and medium stature.
The breeds varied, and included Thoroughbreds, Morgans,
Quarter Horses, and Arabians.

In the United States and Britain, the vogue for applying
principles of selective horse breeding to humans never fully
took hold, thankfully. But in Adolf Hitler's Third Reich, these
ideas would take hold and thrive. Just as Hitler tried to eliminate the Jews for what he perceived as impure bloodlines, Rau
would try to apply that philosophy to horses.

By the time Rau and his entourage departed, they had seen

most of what America's finest horse breeders had to offer. The group returned to a Germany that was teetering on the brink of a modern war.

In just six months, Hitler would invade Poland, where a program was put into place for the "rebuilding of Poland's horse-breeding industry" for the "interest of the German nation." To head up that program, the German Army High Command chose Gustav Rau.

3.

THE POLISH PRINCE

The horses at the Janów Podlaski stud farm in eastern Poland galloped through grassy fields, their silken tails catching the wind like unfurled banners. Inside one of the stud farm's roomy box stalls, at four-thirty a.m. on April 30, 1938, a gray mare (a female horse) delivered a colt onto a thick bed of clean straw. From the moment he struggled upright and his luminous dark brown eyes gazed out upon the world, he attracted notice. His perfect proportions immediately marked him as one of the year's most promising young horses (known as *foals*). On his wide forehead was a large white star. His name, Witez, was fitting for such a fine foal. It was an old Polish word meaning "warrior, chieftain, knight."

Arabian horses were introduced into Poland by the Ottoman Turks in the seventeenth century. By the nineteenth century, wealthy Polish noblemen bred Arabians on their large estates. In 1918, after Bolshevik raids and the trauma of World War I, the count of purebred horses at Janów was zero.

Painstakingly, the staff had taken twenty years to rebuild the stud farm from the ground up. In the spring of 1938, Poland's national breeding program was in full swing, with thirty-three broodmares producing a bumper crop of promising foals.

The stud farm's assistant director, Andrzej Kristalovich, was a quiet young man with a serious angular face. Born in Vienna, Andrzej had grown up around horses, as his father had worked on some of Poland's greatest horse estates. This year, he had proudly looked on as Janów's best stallion (male horse), Ofir, had produced three magnificent colts: Witez and his two half brothers, Witraz (Stained Glass) and Wielki Szjlam (Grand Slam). Kristalovich lingered next to the pasture fence as Witez pranced alongside his mother, Federajca. The dam, a gray mare, had a rare marking called "the bloody shoulder." According to Arabian lore, a mare with this distinctive patch of reddish hair would give birth to horses that would win glory in battle.

Though the Janów stables appeared prosperous and serene, dark clouds of trouble were approaching Poland. By August 1939, the Germans and Russians would sign a nonaggression pact, secretly agreeing that they would not fight over Poland but, instead, divide the country into two spheres of influence—Russia would control the eastern part of the country, and Germany would control the western part. One week later, on September 1, 1939, Germany invaded Poland from the west. Now the Germans were only 150 miles from Janów—and advancing rapidly.

As the threat of a German invasion grew, Kristalovich and the stud farm's small staff huddled together, discussing their plans in worried whispers. To escape on a long overland trip with the horses would be fraught with difficulty. Staying put could be even *more* dangerous, though. After days of wavering, they decided to flee with all of the horses. Their route would take them east over the Bug River, then south toward Romania, where they hoped to find refuge—a trek of more than five hundred overland miles.

On the morning of September 11, 1939, the group set off. The long line of 250 delicate Arabian horses snaked down the narrow, rutted country roads; the percussive sound of their hoofbeats filled the air. Kristalovich led the last group—the most vulnerable, the mares with small frolicking foals at their sides. But when they reached the main east-west highway, the roads were filled with other refugees streaming east away from the German advance. Their fellow travelers shared terrifying tales—the German Air Force had been attacking civilians. The roads were not safe.

Witez was high-spirited, but after hours of trekking, his fatigue was evident. Soon he and his two half brothers were having trouble keeping pace with the older stallions. Some of the youngest foals were dragging behind as their mothers nudged and pushed them along. Before long, a few started to stumble, unable to take another step.

Then disaster struck. The group came upon an enormous Polish military convoy blocking the center of the road. The horses in front panicked at the unexpected sight and started to rear and bolt. In the confusion, a large group of horses broke away. By the time the Janów men gained control and made it through, more than eighty horses had fled—including the three most precious, Witez, Stained Glass, and Grand Slam. Devastated, Kristalovich vowed that once they had reached a safe place, he would return to search out the left-behind horses. He would never get that chance. Somewhere in the forest, Witez wandered alone.

Word had it that the Russians had crossed Poland's eastern border and were heading toward them. Finally, they reached a small wooden bridge that led over the Bug River. Safety from the Germans lay on the other side. To the men of Janów, it seemed as if their worst troubles were behind them.

With renewed hope, they headed toward the village of Kovol, a couple of miles down the road, ready to find a place to rest and shelter the horses. But as they approached, orange flames stood out against the sky: The village was on fire. The sound of artillery boomed deafeningly close. After days of exhausting and dangerous travel, no safer than when they started off, the group could advance no farther.

The men made an agonizing decision: They would return to the stud farm. The entire journey, the loss of the young horses—it had all been for nothing. Thin, limping, and exhausted, the group arrived back at Janów a few days later. There was nothing they could do. The invading army would soon arrive. It was only a question of *when*. On September 25, the waiting ended: Six Russian tanks appeared on the horizon. Janów Podlaski was under Russian occupation.

At first, the Russian troops showed little interest in the horses. Kristalovich and the rest of the staff tried to stay out of sight, emerging only to feed and care for their animals. On the morning of October 5, the men of Janów were relieved to see that the Russians were starting to leave. Their relief soon turned to terror: The soldiers were preparing to take the horses *with* them.

Kristalovich watched in horror as one brutish Russian soldier stomped over to a small gray mare named Nejada. As he attempted to put on her halter, the mare, seeming to understand the danger, lashed out. She struck the Russian, injuring him so severely that he decided to leave her alone. The troops torched the stables as they left, destroying everything they could before leaving.

By the afternoon of October 5, Nejada was the only remaining horse of Janów. The rest of the farm was eerily peaceful. Kristalovich and his staff had done everything they could to protect the horses. Now, just five short weeks since the Russian invasion had started, they were left with nothing but empty stables.

Soon after the Russian soldiers left, another enemy approached from the opposite direction. A shiny black limousine rolled up in front of Janów's tall clock tower. Out stepped the commissioner for horse breeding and stud farming in German-occupied Poland. Gustav Rau had arrived at the stables of Janów Podlaski, ready to take charge. His task was to reassemble the Polish horse-breeding industry—not for the sake of Poland, but for the glory of the Third Reich.

In a cruel and ironic twist, the Nazi invaders—who planned to kick out, enslave, or kill Poland's *human* inhabitants—prized and cared for the well-bred Polish *horses*. Rau immediately set to work restoring Poland's premier stud farm. He set out to find the horses lost along the route when the Poles had tried to flee, and bring them back to German-run Janów. He had two goals for these horses: first, to breed them to keep up with the army's need for transport; and second, to use them to cultivate seized Polish land.

Polish peasants recognized that these horses were their country's treasure. Some had found and hidden the runaways in barns, daubing them with mud to disguise their beauty from Rau and the Germans. But the peasants were afraid of Nazis and didn't hold out long before they handed over the horses when asked. Witez, thin, bedraggled, and pitiably weak, limped back into Janów Podlaski along with his two half brothers, lucky to be among the thirty-odd young horses that were found scattered about the Polish countryside.

The Polish employees of Janów hung back at first, afraid of the German intruders. But Kristalovich's love for his horses was too great for him to stay away long. He stepped forward and volunteered his services as a groom (a stable hand who brushes and feeds the horses). This new role was a huge step down from his previous position, but the best he could do if he wanted to stay with his beloved horses.

Throughout Poland, other stud farms were also being invaded by either Russian or German forces. Either outcome was terrifying, but the Germans tended to look after the horses, which they considered valuable assets. The horses in the pathway of Russian troops, on the other hand, were more likely to be lost or killed—even, in some cases, eaten by desperate and famished soldiers.

Rau watched over an expanding network of German-controlled horse-breeding establishments in Poland. Cruelly, he seized a wealthy Jewish textile merchant's home in Lodz, kicked the man and his family out, and moved himself in. This chief of horse breeding was described by one who knew him as "a man in love with power." He bragged to those in his dominion that he had "a direct line to the führer."

By now, Germany had taken over the Russian-held half of Poland, and with all of Poland's 3.9 million horses under Rau's control, he had an unparalleled opportunity to try to breed the perfect horse for Germany. At Janów Podlaski, the luminous, intelligent, light-footed Witez had not escaped his notice.

But what did Witez see as he gazed at the chaotic world around him? His country of birth was under siege. His father had been carried off like looted treasure by the Russians; his mother had been lost in the turmoil and would never be found. Every morning, he whickered when he saw his groom coming to feed him. He needed what all horses need—care and kindness, fresh oats, clean straw, exercise, a loving word, and a gentle pat.

4.

RAU'S DOMINION

Debica, Poland, 1942

In 1942, the Nazis were at the height of their powers as Hitler's stranglehold stretched across Europe. Many lavished money and attention on breeding farms, horse shows, and races that they entertained themselves with during their occupation of Poland. The Third Reich had created a vast kingdom of horses, and Rau was its emperor.

By now, three years had passed since Gustav Rau first arrived at Janów Podlaski, restoring the stud farm and finding the lost horses. His authority had spread out across Poland, with fourteen stud farms and more than seventy employees. The German Army still relied heavily on horses to transport heavy artillery and supplies—increasing their number of horses was a priority. They were churning through horses at an astonishing rate and demanded six thousand fresh ones per month to replace those killed or lost to disease. In 1938, the peacetime German Army possessed only 183,000 horses (including donkeys).

By 1945, the Germans would employ 2.7 *million* horses in the war effort, more than double the number used in World War I.

Gustav Rau had limitless funds at his disposal to travel all over Europe to purchase—or seize—horses characterized by highly refined pedigrees; he was hoping to capture their "pure blood" for his mission to create the "perfect" German warhorse. Soon his interest began to center more and more on the Lipizzaners. He sent one of his aides on a buying mission to Yugoslavia, where he procured for the Reich all of the Lipizzaner stock from the royal Yugoslavian and Croatian stud farms. Rau sent some of these horses to a stud farm in Czechoslovakia for safekeeping. Others were fanned out across Poland and the Ukraine.

Rau's aide, Rudolf Lessing, toured the vast domain alongside him, assisting in veterinary matters. Lessing had grown up on a farm, clambering on horseback as soon as he could walk. As a young man, he was persuaded by the Nazi rhetoric and accepted Hitler's aims without questioning them. Against his father's wishes, he joined the Hitler Youth. Later, Lessing would characterize his enthusiasm for Hitler as inexplicable.

As a veterinary officer, Lessing was most occupied with animals. He had never seen Nazi leadership up close. This all changed when Gustav Rau recruited him to work in his horse-breeding domain. For the young veterinarian, it was a dream job that took him all over Poland, including frequent visits to Janów Podlaski. The friendly face of Witez was a familiar sight as he toured the stallion barns.

But as he later described in his memoirs, it was not possible to work in Poland without realizing the horrific truth of
what was going on there. One afternoon, heading home after
a full day caring for horses, Rudolf Lessing looked out from a
train that was paused in the station. He was heading back to
his home base, located at one of Rau's stud farms in Debica,
in eastern Poland near the Ukraine. In his German Army uniform, Lessing was a tall, handsome man with light blue eyes,
sandy hair, and a long, chiseled face. From his window, he could
see black ashes spewing into the air. Above the busy platform,
the sign read "Auschwitz." Beyond heavy barbed-wire fences, a
huge German industrial complex spread out toward the horizon. Lessing knew that at this "agricultural station," a gruesome
truth was unfolding.

"They're gassing the Jews. So many people know what's
going on." He had tried to explain to his father once, but his
father had refused to believe him.

If the Germans win this war, there is no God Almighty, he
thought as the train pulled away.

Lessing had made it his life's work to care for those who
could not speak for themselves. For years, his quiet ways and
deft hands had soothed and quieted panicked horses that had
been put in harm's way by humans. Lessing had a natural sympathy for those who could not protect themselves—yet now he
found himself working within a system that made brutality its
central goal.

Lessing soon realized that Rau was not encouraging Polish
horse breeding for the benefit of the horses *or* the Polish nation. It was only for the glorification of the Third Reich. While

human beings were being transported in cattle cars, horses moved about in plush padded train cars. After working with Rau for under a year, Lessing had given up believing in the Nazi cause. His vow of loyalty, in his own mind, was no longer to the führer but only to the horses.

5.

THE SPANISH RIDING SCHOOL OF VIENNA

Vienna, Austria, May 1942

Neapolitano Africa floated across the sand floor of the Spanish Riding School in Vienna. Enormous arched windows bathed the Lipizzaner stallion's all-white coat in a golden glow. The Riding School was one of Vienna's architectural marvels. A palace built in 1736 by the powerful Habsburg monarchs, it had the express purpose of showcasing the grand jewel of their empire: the equestrian arts.

From the saddle, Olympian and bronze medalist Alois Podhajsky, clad in tall black riding boots, made a series of minute adjustments, communicating with the stallion in a language— small shifts of weight, light contact on the reins—that they both spoke fluently. Ever since he had trained Africa, Podhajsky and the horse had shared a special, unbreakable bond.

Africa's ears cocked back. He was concentrating. With no obvious cue from the rider, the stallion sank back on his haunches and began to circle around his hind hooves, which continued to canter in place: a movement known as a *pirouette.*

Around them in the arena, other uniformed riders practiced diligently astride similar stallions.

To this day, each stallion at the Spanish Riding School is branded with an imperial crown. At age three and a half, they begin their training before launching into routines that take years to perfect. Training proceeds in three stages:

First is *straight-line training,* where a young horse is taught the basic paces (walk, trot, and canter) and learns to carry a rider on his back.

Next is *campagne school,* where horses learn balance while developing the muscles and flexibility needed for the higher-level movements; this allows them to shift their center of balance to their haunches in order to free up the forelegs' action.

The final stage is the *haute école,* or high school, which addresses the most complex movements, such as the slow-motion elevated trot named *passage,* and the prancing in place called *piaffe.* They are among the most difficult in the equestrian domain.

A few of the exceptionally talented stallions learn the most difficult movements of all: the "airs above the ground." When performing, these stallions raise their forelegs off the ground entirely, balancing only on the hind legs. Some do a leap and kick called a *capriole;* others, a magnificent jump known as the *courbette.*

For centuries, these beautiful creatures performed exclusively for the eyes of the royals. Until World War I, that is. In 1918, the monarchs and their empire were overthrown, and the school seemed doomed to fall into oblivion since their usual audience and patrons weren't there. Slowly, throughout the 1920s and 1930s, the school rebuilt an audience to stay in business, under the direction of the *Austrian* Ministry of Agriculture. Then, in 1938, when Austria was annexed by Nazi Germany, the school was put under the control of the *German* Army High Command.

When the Germans offered Alois Podhajsky a post under the new military leadership, the Austrian made a conflicted compromise: He would save the horses and the school even if it meant collaborating with the Germans. That meant that now he answered to the German Army, and to Hitler.

Unlike the horses at Janów Podlaski in Poland, the white Lipizzaner stallions that lived at the Spanish Riding School in Vienna had thrived since the Nazi occupation of Austria. They had been lavished with attention and taken on tours to perform for crowds around Europe. The Germans clearly understood that the beloved white stallions of Vienna boosted the morale of the occupied city.

The school was flourishing, yet Alois Podhajsky was worried. Since 1939, Gustav Rau had been moving horses, including Lipizzaners, like chess pieces all over the German-occupied territories. He had not yet interfered with the running of the Spanish Riding School. But would that last? Podhajsky had heard a rumor that Rau planned to move the Lipizzaners from Piber—where all of the school's stallions were bred and raised before being sent to Vienna—to a location *outside* Austria. He wanted to move *Austria's* crown jewels out of the country.

In July 1942, Podhajsky set off for Piber to see what was happening firsthand. Upon arrival, he was struck by the beauty of the place. The valley was studded with wildflowers and sparkling streams. The air felt crystal clear. Walking through the stables, he knew each of the mares by name, and, in turn, all of them recognized the serious man whose pockets were always stuffed with sugar cubes.

The way the Lipizzaners were raised and cared for in their early years was quite particular. While most purebred horses lived in carefully kept stables, these young stallions galloped freely against the picturesque and rugged background of the Styrian Alps. Podhajsky believed strongly in the importance of the natural surroundings to the development of the young Lipizzaners. The very idea of their being moved disturbed him greatly. After returning to Vienna, Podhajsky sent a letter to Berlin, pleading with Rau not to move the mares from Piber. The conditions of climate and terrain, he wrote, were ideal for nurturing these special horses.

Rau received Podhajsky's letter but did not respond. He considered the Austrian's arguments backward and unscientific. In essence, Rau and Podhajsky were on different sides of the nature-versus-nurture debate. Podhajsky believed that without the special nurture of the Piber stud farm, the Lipizzaner would lose something crucial; to Rau, like the Nazis, only their pedigree mattered.

In early October, unbeknownst to Podhajsky, Rau sent the entire bloodstock of the Piber stud farm—stallions, mares, and foals—onto specially designed train cars. Their destination: a much larger stud farm located in the village of Hostau in the western Bohemian region of Czechoslovakia. The Hostau farm was spacious and well maintained, with plenty of room for expansion. Rau's big plan was to send *all* the Lipizzaners—from Lipica, several stud farms in Yugoslavia, and Piber—to this single location, far from the war zone.

For the first time, these Lipizzaners were leaving Austria.

By the time the news reached Podhajsky in Vienna, the stables at Piber were empty. Podhajsky was devastated. What would happen to these Austrian horses if the Germans ever lost control of their territories? If Hitler's Reich came crashing down, who would be there to protect them? The Czech locals had no special loyalty to the Lipizzaner breed. They might not even be familiar with the Spanish Riding School.

Podhajsky went to Hostau to visit his beloved horses, and there he found that the mares and foals had arrived in good condition. But to his horror, he discovered that Gustav Rau had plans for the Lipizzaners. Rau had no interest in the Lipizzaners as a breed—he wanted to engineer the perfect warhorse. As such, he was going to experiment with "linebreeding," a practice in which close relatives are bred to each other to reshape and accentuate certain characteristics in the animal. He was going to use Austria's greatest natural treasure as his guinea pigs until there were none left.

The horrors of all-out war intensified around the world that year. In America, President Roosevelt signed Executive Order 9066, which authorized moving Americans of Japanese descent into relocation centers. Nazi leaders met in secret at an event later known as the Wannsee Conference, where they put into place what was called "the final solution": the extermination of the Jews of Europe. In 1934, there were 176,034 Jews in Vienna. By 1941, 130,000 of them had fled the city. Of the 65,000 Viennese Jews who were sent to concentration camps, only about 2,000 survived.

As these catastrophes unfolded, Podhajsky's attention to his horses remained single-minded. He was determined to meet with Rau in person to present his case. Arriving in Berlin, he entered the towering headquarters of the German Army High Command. Podhajsky was nervous. While renowned as an equestrian, he was not known for his particular expertise in breeding horses. To make matters worse, he was aware that the Germans looked down on him as an Austrian.

The two men parried back and forth, passionately arguing their positions. The Austrian cautioned that taking the horses out of their habitat was careless, and that breeding mares too young would prove disastrous. Finally an agreement was made that Rau should avoid breeding the younger Austrian mares. But the Lipizzaners were to remain at Hostau. Returning the mares to Piber—or anywhere else in Austria—was out of the question.

Podhajsky prepared to play his desperate final hand. In just a few weeks, on November 29, 1942, the Spanish Riding School would be putting on a gala evening performance to which high-ranking Nazis were invited. Gustav Rau would be there. On this night, Podhajsky was to debut a spectacular new program: a formal dance called a quadrille performed with twelve stallions. In these highly choreographed sequences, the horses moved so close to one another that just a few inches of error would cause them to fall out of line or collide. Surely if the German over-lords could see the Lipizzaners perform such intricate moves, they would recognize that the horses had a special purpose that was worthy of preservation. Perhaps they would change their minds about breeding experiments at Hostau.

It came time for the performance. With Podhajsky in the lead, the twelve mounted riders from the Spanish Riding School entered the hall in single file. The music of Mozart swelled over the loudspeakers as the horses trotted and cantered with the precision of a military marching band in the intricate and difficult quadrille. Finally, the horses formed a single line again, halting in the center of the arena in perfect formation, twelve abreast.

The applause seemed to go on and on as Podhajsky and the stallions filed out of the riding hall. Rau had clearly been impressed with the performance, but deep down, Podhajsky knew the man's mind was made up. Sadly, he walked through the aisles of the stables. His friends greeted him with a chorus of neighs, stomping feet, and friendly whickers. His own mount, Neapolitano Africa, always seemed to know what he was thinking—in the horse's wise eyes, Podhajsky could read the language of friendship. The control of the Lipizzaner mares and foals had slipped from his grasp, but he vowed to redouble his determination to protect the stallions at all costs.

6.

THE HIDDEN STUD FARM

Beyond the serene green pastures of the Hostau stud farm, golden valleys stretched toward distant mountains. Czechoslovakia's Böhmerwald, or Bohemian Forest, served as more than just a beautiful backdrop for the farm; it formed a barrier between Germany and Austria and had withstood invasion and attack for centuries. It was here that Rau had brought the Lipizzaners from Piber, Austria, as well as the finest Arabians from Janów, including Witez. Even in the middle of a war, the farm was deceptively tranquil.

Once a multicultural region where Czechs, Germans, and Jews lived side by side in peace, Bohemia had turned into a firm cornerstone of Hitler's Third Reich. Local Czechs and Jews had either fled or been heartlessly shoved out. Those who remained had been forcibly transported to concentration camps.

Just as Hitler aimed to eliminate "impure strains" and combine the different Germanic groups into a single "Aryan race" of people, so Rau planned to use the science of selective breeding to erase the individual differences characterizing the several strains of purebred Lipizzaners and replace them with an identical mold: pure white and suited for military use.

As head of the Polish stud farm administration, Rau had increased the number of stallions, mares, and foals born in Poland year upon year, feeding them to the war. Rau envisioned hundreds of thousands of purebred Lipizzaners fanning out across the German empire, as reliable and identical as cars. Yet unlike cars, horses—living, breathing animals that require exercise, food, and care—could not be fabricated like nuts and bolts in a factory.

With a modern understanding of genetic inheritance, animal breeders now know too well the problems with breeding animals too closely, which can leave animals susceptible to disease or inherited genetic defects. But this modern understanding of genetics was not available to Rau, and he was determined to breed family members together.

When Darwin published his theory of evolution in 1859, he knew that traits were passed from parent to offspring, though he did not know *how*. The father of the science of genetic inheritance was Gregor Mendel, an Augustinian friar whose experiments with pea plants, published in 1866, provided the first demonstration of the principles of inheritance. But until the late nineteenth century, scientists continued to believe that offspring could inherit characteristics acquired by parents from their environment—for example, giraffes elongated their necks by reaching into high branches for food, and these longer necks then were passed along to their offspring. By contrast, modern science knows that characteristics such as the giraffe's long neck do not come about from anything an individual giraffe chooses to do. Instead, they come about very slowly, over long periods of time, hundreds of thousands of years, as animals adapt to their environments.

But Rau did not have access to the insights of modern science. In his approach to horse breeding, Rau followed the theory of German scientist August Weismann (1834–1914). Weismann thought that inherited traits were not changeable or influenced by their surroundings. He believed that children were born with the exact same qualities as their parents—if a parent was lazy or uneducated, then the child would be the same. And in contrast, if a parent was rich and hardworking, then the child must be too. This theory supported the Nazi argument that no matter how assimilated a Jewish person might *seem*, every Jewish baby was born with certain unchanging (and, in the bigots' view, negative) characteristics that could be passed from one generation to the next. Weismann entirely denied the influence of nurture or environment on inherited traits. We now understand that complex characteristics, such as intelligence, honor, personality, and character, are not inherited in the same way that simple qualities, such as hair and eye color, can be passed from parent to child. The racialist idea that certain groups of people have good or bad qualities that are passed along from parent to child has been disproven. People are not born with a blueprint, and the Nazi way of thinking has long since been discredited.

But Rau was limited by old-fashioned beliefs about how inheritance worked. He believed that purebred horses needed to be protected from corrupt outside influences, such as "mixed blood." He had the radical idea that breeding horses that were close family relations—father to daughter, mother to son—a discredited practice known as linebreeding—would result in better offspring. Not understanding the dangers of line-breeding, Rau believed that increasing "purity" would improve quality—and finally reach his standard for a "perfect" horse.

To lead this enterprise on the ground, Rau had chosen another personal protégé, forty-six-year-old Czech-born German Hubert Rudofsky, one of Czechoslovakia's foremost experts on equine breeding.

Rudofsky had learned to ride at the age of ten. When World War I broke out, seventeen-year-old Rudofsky had eagerly enlisted in the Austrian cavalry. Once Germany occupied Czechoslovakia, Rudofsky was called up to serve in the German armed forces known as the Wehrmacht. Now a colonel, he was over six feet tall, a bachelor known for his dapper manner, immaculate dress, and knowledge of horses.

Hubert Rudofsky was an expert at carriage driving. He could drive a four-in-hand, one of the equestrian world's most rarefied skills. Traditionally, four harnessed horses pulling a heavy carriage required two drivers, one to control each pair of reins. *Four-in-hand* refers to the four reins, one for each horse, that a driver controls in a single hand—the left. With the right, the driver holds a long carriage whip anchored between the thumb and little finger, freeing up the middle three fingers to control the reins during turns.

Rau pulled Rudofsky away from his assignment in Poland to serve in his home region of Bohemia, where he would assume the job of overseeing the Reich's greatest equine treasures: the Lipizzaners at Hostau.

Rudofsky returned to Czechoslovakia to find his home much changed. The stud farm of Hostau was in tip-top shape, but the war had fractured and splintered the quiet village. When Rudofsky returned to Bohemia, now "cleansed" of its ethnic minorities, he found his homeland sadly diminished.

Within Rudofsky's own family, sentiments toward the Third Reich were bitterly divided. Privately, Rudofsky disdained the Nazis. But in his eyes, he had no choice but to don the Wehrmacht uniform; the civilian horse-breeding system he worked within had been swallowed whole by the German Army. In the eyes of the Czech citizens who had been chased from their homes by Nazis, he and his German-speaking compatriots were traitors.

Being closer to home did have one advantage for Rudofsky. Though he did not have any children of his own, he had a ten-year-old nephew, Ulli, whom he adored as his own child. Rudofsky made it a point to keep watch on the young boy. The boy's father, Rudofsky's brother, had not been heard from in some time, and in German-occupied Czechoslovakia, it was fair to fear the worst. Rudofsky stopped by his sister-in-law's house often to have dinner with Ulli and quiz him on his arithmetic tables.

In the winter of 1943, Rudofsky arranged for Ulli and his sister, Susi, to visit the majestic horses at Hostau. Like something out of a fairy tale, a carriage pulled by two snow-white horses appeared in front of the children's house. The driver opened the door and tucked Ulli and Susi into warm blankets sewn together like sleeping bags. From inside the snug carriage,

the children could see the snowy, rolling fields. After petting the
beautiful horses and seeing their uncle expertly tend to them,
they were left with an indelible impression of the seemingly
magical animals.

The day-to-day routine in Hostau was steeped in centuries-
old tradition. Every Monday, Rudofsky inspected all the horses
with the utmost care and kindness. Up and down the long aisles
of the stables, grooms fussed with their charges, making sure
every hair was perfect, from the tips of the horses' well-formed
ears to the very ends of their silky tails. Details of each horse
were recorded in the voluminous stud-farm books: health, temperament, soundness, and physical characteristics. This information was passed up the line to Gustav Rau, who made the
decisions about pairing mares and stallions.

During 1944, Alois Podhajsky and his wife, Verena, visited
Hostau to see the Lipizzaner mares from Piber. Verena Podhajsky, a friendly woman with curly chin-length hair, would greet
the horses in their pastures and socialize with the stud farm's
staff. But Podhajsky's relationship with Colonel Rudofsky was
chilly. Podhajsky was eager to interfere with Rau's plans, convinced that the Austrian mares should not be subjected to any
breeding experiments. Rudofsky did not appreciate Podhajsky's
desire to meddle in the breeding farm; after all, he had no choice
but to follow Rau's commands.

One thing is clear: Rau's plan to increase the number of specially bred Lipizzaners was successful. By 1944, the pastures
around Hostau were filled with placid white broodmares with
frolicking dark-coated foals at their sides. The first of Rau's

new breed of Lipizzaners were being born, though it was too soon to tell what the outcome would be; it would take years to fully evaluate the performance of these close-bred newborns, and several generations before selective mating could substantially alter the offspring.

7.

PODHAJSKY'S CHOICE

Vienna, 1943

After a season of rigorous training at the Spanish Riding School, Neapolitano Africa and the other horses took some well-earned rest at the spacious Lainzer Tiergarten, the Lipizzaners' summer stables on the outskirts of Vienna. In this peaceful setting, the hardworking stallions relaxed and took long rides through the countryside.

The time was nearing when the school traditionally returned to Vienna for the winter season. But 1943 was not shaping up to be an ordinary year. The tide of war had started to turn against the Germans. Allied bombers were dropping enormous explosives on German cities. Many feared that Vienna might be next.

Podhajsky knew that his first duty was to keep the stallions safe. The problem was that he was not sure *how* to. One view was that the school should stay at the summer stables. Far from the city, it would be an unlikely target for Allied bombers. Another view was that it would be best to go back to Vienna, as was traditional. After all, the horses were a symbol of Austrian identity. If they failed to return, would not the citizens start to lose hope?

Maybe he was an idealist, but Podhajsky could not believe that the Allies would drop bombs on Vienna, home of some of the world's most important cultural treasures. He and the horses returned to Vienna.

A few months later, the situation had grown worse. Allied bombers were getting closer every day. Despite the grim conditions in the city, within the walls of the riding school, Podhajsky had managed to maintain strict discipline. The horses and riders carried on with their exacting training regimen. The stallions' performances kept attracting more and more crowds. Podhajsky sensed that after a few hours spent in the magical presence of the horses, people returned home with just a little bit of hope. But each day, the world seemed to grow grimmer— even the stallions could not hold back the dark curtain forever.

On March 17, 1944, Podhajsky's worst fears were realized: American B-17s appeared over Vienna. The bombings had begun.

By summertime, the white stallions had learned to recognize the air raid signal. Each time a bomb struck, Africa cowered, trying to escape the loud explosions coming from above. To Podhajsky, it seemed that Africa and the stallions had a peculiar expression on their faces, as if saying, "How perplexing humans are!" Ultimately, the responsibility for their safety rested entirely with him, and as the raids grew more frequent, he had to admit that the horses could not stay here, even if their performances helped boost morale. The Lipizzaners could not be expected to dance through air strikes and keep alive the illusion that everything was all right. The danger was too great.

When Podhajsky met with a German city official to plead for permission to take the horses out of Vienna, he was told that if the Lipizzaners left the city, people would lose heart. Podhajsky was all too aware of that, and he sensed an underlying threat in the German official's words. At this point in Nazi-occupied Austria, anything that sounded like admitting defeat—even fleeing a city that was being bombed—was considered treason and would mean serious punishment.

Secretly, throughout that fall, he packed up every single belonging of the Spanish Riding School, even having the enormous crystal chandeliers disassembled and boxed up. He redoubled his efforts to find a safer place far from the city that could accommodate so many horses. At last, he discovered a large castle in Upper Austria, in the village of St. Martin im Innkreis, that had stables big enough to hold his seventy-five horses. The castle was owned by Countess Gertrud Arco auf Valley. There would be room for all of Podhajsky's stallions, as well as for him, his wife, and a few grooms. But an increasingly desperate Podhajsky could not get the authorities to let him leave. No transport was available. All trucks were being used for military purposes.

Podhajsky had a thought: Even if his pleas to save the horses were not working, perhaps he could make a case to move the rest of the precious artifacts—saddles, bridles, and artwork— from the school. When he was granted permission, he made an additional request: Could he use space on the truck to move some of the horses to the empty stables in St. Martin? Instead of presenting this move as the riding school leaving the city, he said that it was simply to ease overcrowding at the stables in Vienna.

To his relief, a city official finally agreed. In this way, in January and February, Podhajsky managed to ship small groups of horses to safety, so that by late February 1945, only fifteen stallions and a small number of riders remained. He had fulfilled his obligation to keep the riding school in the city while making sure that a good number of the horses were out of harm's way.

The bombings intensified. On March 7, the Allies crossed the Remagen bridge over the Rhine into eastern Germany. Meanwhile, the Russians were pressing in from the east. Podhajsky desperately needed to evacuate the remaining fifteen horses. There was no choice but to, at last, close down the riding school entirely. All that was needed was permission from the district official, also known as the *Gauleiter*, of Vienna.

Podhasky braced himself before visiting the *Gauleiter* in his villa. Wasting no time, he stated his business. "Due to the danger to the horses posed by the air raids, it is necessary to remove the horses from the city *immediately.*"

The *Gauleiter* looked upset. "If the Lipizzaners are seen leaving the city, it will make the citizens feel as if they are in a hopeless position," he argued.

Podhajsky avoided stating the obvious—that the citizens of Vienna *were* in a hopeless position. The only question now was whether the Russians would invade or the Americans and British would flatten the city with bombs.

"The stallions are irreplaceable. They need to be evacuated

to a safer location immediately," Podhajsky stated firmly. To re-move the remaining fifteen stallions from a wartime city under siege would be a grand undertaking; he would never pull it off without the agreement of the man who stood before him.

"It is not easy for me to agree to the evacuation," the *Gau-leiter* said, then paused. "But I love them too much to leave them in danger any longer . . ."

Podhajsky felt his knees almost buckle in relief, but he re-sponded only with a curt nod. The horses inspired people to love them, even this coldhearted and brutal Nazi. Effectively, the stallions had won their own freedom. But Podhajsky knew that his ordeal was far from over. It would be a long, difficult trek to get the horses safely away while air raids bombarded the city daily.

8.

HORSES IN PERIL

In the spring of 1944, while Podhajsky struggled to protect his stallions in Austria, the war was creeping closer to the German-controlled Janów Podlaski stud farm in Poland. Janów was just a few miles from Russia—which put the farm dangerously close to the fighting.

In early May, the stud farm received orders from Gustav Rau. Nine of Janów's best Arabians would be shipped to Hostau, where, with the careful movements of a chess master, Rau had been strategically moving the very finest horses. Among those chosen by Rau was the most valuable of all of the young stallions—Witez.

In the stable under the tall clock tower, one of Janów's most devoted grooms, Jan Ziniewicz, moved with slow steps and a heavy heart from stall to stall, speaking a soft word to each horse as he passed. He had a quiet, sympathetic manner that the horses responded to. When he approached Witez, the Polish horse greeted him with a nudge. Gloomily, Ziniewicz clipped a lead rope to the stallion's halter and guided him out of the stable. Today was the day when Witez and nine other Arabians would board a train bound for Hostau, Czechoslovakia.

Ziniewicz had been assigned to watch out for the horses' well-being during the nine-day train ride, which took them west through Warsaw and Lodz, then south toward Prague. When they finally arrived at Hostau, the groom found familiar faces from Poland—the stud master Rudofsky and the kindly young veterinarian Lessing, both of whom had been frequent visitors at Janów. Still, the familiar faces offered only fleeting comfort: Ziniewicz had to say a hurried goodbye to his horses, then, following orders, turned around to go back to Janów, leaving the pride of Poland behind on foreign soil.

Settled at Hostau, Witez fared well. Hay and grain were plentiful, and the stable was comfortable. Far from Poland, these horses were no longer in immediate danger. But the Polish staff of Janów Podlaski could not believe that their treasured horse had slipped from their grasp. Now Witez was far away, on a farm in a foreign country controlled by Germans. Nobody knew if he would ever return. Of Ofir's three greatest sons of 1938, only Stained Glass and Grand Slam, Witez's half brothers, remained.

Fights between the German Wehrmacht and the Soviet partisans worsened. In May 1944, a German bomb landed on Janów, partially destroying one of the stallion barns. Fortunately, the horses were out at pasture and none was hurt. In late June, Rau finally announced that the entire Janów farm would have to be evacuated. This time, luckily, the ninety-six horses would not have to flee on foot. Rau had arranged train transport to Sohland, a small German city several hundred miles to the west. A retired cavalry officer would open his stables to the refugees and take over responsibility for the horses.

Late at night, in the quiet of his home, the Assistant Director of Janów, Andrzej Kristalovich, and his wife discussed the plan in anxious whispers. Traveling with their young daughter would be dangerous, and venturing west toward Germany was marching into the jaws of the enemy. But ending up in the hands of the Russians was also terrifying. What would happen if the horses were killed—or worse, eaten? The Russian Army was huge, and starving, and known for killing and eating any animal in its path. In the end, Kristalovich and his wife agreed to travel with the horses. He had been entrusted with safeguarding Poland's national treasure. His primary duty was to stick with the horses. They would go.

In Sohland, the horses were out of immediate danger, but all was not well. The crowded conditions, the lack of staff, and the scarcity of good-quality food in these borrowed stables had left the beautiful Arabians in pitiful shape.

Conditions kept deteriorating. There were barely enough men to care for the Arabians, and both space and fodder were growing short. Kristalovich and Ziniewicz did everything they could to help, but—with the arrival of hundreds of other desperate men and horses—the estate had been pushed beyond its capacity. There were too many horses crowded into one place.

Just twelve months earlier, these horses had been the best kept in all of Europe, and now their condition was pitiful—cramped stabling, untended hooves, respiratory infections, dull coats.

Finally, Gustav Rau arrived in Sohland to take charge. He pared down the horse herd until only the very best remained. With pleading eyes, the bedraggled horses seemed to watch warily as Rau made his rounds. Kristalovich and Ziniewicz had tended to Witez's brothers carefully, currying them until they shone and eking out extra rations of grain. Among the worn-down lot, they looked better than most.

Only the horses Rau selected were allowed to stay at Sohland. He instructed the staff to give the remaining magnificent Arabians to locals. Gustav Rau took great pains to tell the new owners that the horses were being given "as a loan to fighting troops and soldiers, to be returned after the war." One by one, some of Poland's most priceless horses were led down the country lane and disappeared from sight. None of these Arabians would ever be recovered for Poland. Once again, the two Polish horsemen could only watch as the number of their purebreds shrank.

By February 1945, Sohland was no longer safe. They would flee on foot to Torgau, a large army remounting station about ninety miles away. The plan was to head first to the city of Dresden, then continue to Torgau after a few days of rest. The stallions would set off first. Kristalovich would follow slowly with the most vulnerable group—the mares and foals.

Along the narrow, hilly country lanes, an icy rain soaked

through their wool coats and blankets. Wind whipped through the men's drenched outer garments, through the horses' manes and dull, scraggly winter coats. Mares with swollen bellies trudged along, heavy-footed, their heads hanging. By this point, millions of people in the eastern part of Germany's realm were trying to flee before the Russian Army's arrival. Wagons, cars, trucks, gasoline—all were scarce.

As they approached the city of Dresden on the night of February 13, their timing could not have been worse. Of course, the Janów men were nowhere near a radio as they trudged through the rain. If they had been, they would have heard a Dresden announcer interrupt the nightly program to warn people of Allied bombs: "*Achtung! Achtung!* An attack is coming! Go to your cellars at once!"

In the center of Dresden, people hurried underground. On the city's outskirts, where masses of refugees, including the group from Janów, were milling around, most never received the message. Besides, there was nowhere to hide. Ammunition lit up the sky over the old city. A few moments later, a crushing roar rumbled above.

The stallions squealed in panic. In a moment, their high-pitched sounds were drowned out by the unceasing roar of planes overhead. Unwittingly, the men had ridden the horses directly into one of the biggest air attacks of the war: the Allied bombing of Dresden, during which 722 heavy bombers from the British Royal Air Force and 527 from the United States Army Air Forces dropped 3,900 tons of explosives in two waves about three hours apart, resulting in a firestorm that destroyed most of central Dresden.

No one had believed that Dresden—like Vienna, with its magnificent architecture, arts, and culture—would be a target of the Allied bombs. Now, as flames engulfed the city, the horizon turned fiery orange, and a thick cloud of smoke obscured the sky. The stallions panicked, rearing and lashing out, crazily trying to escape the noise and intense heat. Men and horses fled in all directions, but the fire rained down everywhere—there was nowhere to run.

Jan Ziniewicz focused every bit of his strength on the two stallions in his charge, Witez's half brothers. Flashes of light revealed a terrifying picture—craters and flames, people on fire, horses rearing and running in all directions, and still the awful sound of bombs, like a freight train running through the sky. Stained Glass and Grand Slam strained hard against their halters. Their eyes whitened in fear. Sweat beaded up on Ziniewicz's brow, but he clenched his teeth and held on to their leads.

Then, all of a sudden, the unholy roar ended. Ziniewicz and his two horses had made it through the bombing unscathed. But he could not even see half of the group—all around him was a mass of wailing people and charred remains.

Kristalovich, traveling with the mares and foals, was half a day behind. When his group arrived along the road just at the city's outskirts, he came upon the corpses of seventeen of his beloved stallions and began to weep. At last, he came upon Jan Ziniewicz. The two men embraced. Together, they tried to round up the survivors.

Kristalovich and Ziniewicz had no time to focus on the heartbreak of their losses, as every waking moment was taken up by caring for the surviving Arabians. Eventually, they found shelter still farther west, in Nettlelau, Germany, where they were able to ride out the war. More than two hundred purebred Arabians had fled Janów in January 1944. There were fewer than fifty remaining. Kristalovich and Ziniewicz had no idea what fate had befallen the few prized stallions and mares selected to be sent to Hostau—they could only hope for the best.

9.

THE ESCAPE

Spanish Riding School, Vienna, March 6, 1945

Rumors swirled that the Russians would arrive within days. The time had come to escape from the Spanish Riding School with the last fifteen Lipizzaner stallions. Among this final group were Podhajsky's two personal mounts, Africa and his barn mate, Pluto. They had stayed back with their owner to continue daily training.

Two large cargo trucks pulled up outside the riding school, ready to transport the remaining few horses to the train station. Podhajsky's wife, Verena, had packed up their belongings. When the last stallion was loaded, the imperial stables stood empty and eerily silent for the first time in more than three centuries.

The group's route would take them across the country to their final destination: St. Martin im Innkreis, the small town in Upper Austria. On the train, Podhajsky recalled his last view of his beloved riding school. Several of the windows were papered over with cardboard after shattering during the bombings. The crystal chandeliers were gone; their absence made the riding hall seem more ordinary. Despite his relief that he had found a way to get the horses out of the city, Podhajsky was melancholy. Never in the long history of the riding school had the horses fled the city. Would they ever come back? At last, every one of his horses was headed toward safety, but their institution might not survive.

After numerous lengthy delays, the train finally made progress as far as Amstetten, about fifty miles west of Vienna. Podhajsky circled back to the horses' cars, where the animals stood, fidgety but patient. Their eyes were so trusting, showing an enduring faith in their master. He fished in his ever-present leather pouch and fed sugar lumps to each stallion, whispering comforting words, trying to project a confidence that he did not feel. He lingered next to Africa for an extra moment, thanking him for his patience in this trying situation. The animal's dark eyes were so wise and understanding, even in this most gloomy predicament.

Air raid sirens were already wailing when the train pulled into Linz train station. A transport officer jumped up and yelled orders: "Passengers disembark and go directly to the air raid shelters." His shouts rang through the ruckus.

People scurried frantically toward the shelters as the sirens wailed. There was no way to get the horses off the transport that quickly, nor was there anywhere for them to go. Instead of joining the throng, Podhajsky headed toward the car where Pluto and Africa were confined. Ignoring the screech of the air raid signal and the mad gestures of the stationmaster, Podhajsky climbed into the train car with his stallions. Without saying a word, Verena and the grooms loyally followed him.

Even before the bombs began, they could feel the train car vibrating. Soon the ground was shaking and the air was filled with deafening booms. Pluto huddled up against Africa. Unable to flee, the horses could only snort or paw the floor. Fear filled their eyes. Their nostrils flared and their breath trumpeted in fear. Podhajsky murmured reassurances, but in truth, he too was terrified. The only comfort was that they were together. Earth-splitting booms ripped through the air, each one seeming like the one that would tear them apart.

Podhajsky would never underestimate a horse's courage or loyalty. All he could do was hold his wife and show his horses that even in this terrible moment, he would not desert them either.

Bombs fell like rain from the sky for what felt like a long time. When the all clear sounded, they cowered for a moment longer in silence. Then everything whirred back into motion. Podhajsky felt the bump and jostle as the locomotive hitched up their cars and pulled them the short distance into the Linz station.

Before any of them even had time to breathe a sigh of relief, the sirens ripped through the air again. In a frenzy, Podhajsky realized that they were about to be plunged back into the same terror they had just escaped.

By nightfall, they had survived two more raids, and the sky was bloodred from the burning of so many fires. At last, around midnight, the train pulled off the main line onto the northerly local line that would carry them the rest of the way to their destination. The air raid sirens ceased.

✦ ✦ ✦

Podhajsky, Verena, the grooms, Pluto, Africa, and the thirteen other stallions spent four days together on that train before arriving at the small village of St. Martin. The quiet country roads were a stark contrast to the inferno from which they had escaped. Podhajsky managed a smile as he saw his stallions sniffing the air and looking around at their new surroundings. The exhausted group of horses and men walked up the narrow country lane, greeted by the chirping of birds and lowing of cows in distant pastures.

When they arrived at the estate's spacious stables, the stallions that were already there whinnied greetings, joyous to rediscover their friends from Vienna after the long separation. At last, the seventy-five stallions of the Spanish Riding School were gathered safely under one roof.

The sounds of guns and falling bombs still echoed in his ears as Podhajsky led Africa and Pluto into their stalls for the night. The new stables were so much less grand than their home in Vienna, yet Podhajsky couldn't help but feel that the horses somehow understood. At least no bombs fell on this isolated village.

By now, Podhajsky knew that the war would end with Germany's defeat. Beyond that, he could not predict the future. The stallions would live, but without the survival of the institutions that supported them—the Spanish Riding School and the Piber stud farm—where could they return after the war?

By March 1945, communications in the German Reich had grown undependable. News from Hostau, where the mares were stabled, was spotty. Podhajsky had lost all contact with

Rau and suspected that his empire had lost its power—even perhaps been shattered. The Russians were advancing from the east, with Hostau in their direct path, in which case the mares and foals would be in great danger. The Russians had been ruthless in their treatment of horses—drafting them for war use, shooting the uncooperative ones, and worse yet, slaughtering livestock, including horses, to feed their hungry armies.

If the Russians arrived in Hostau, Podhajsky had no doubt that the horses would be lost to Austria and might very well lose their lives. And there was nothing he could do about it. The fate of the mares was completely out of his hands.

PART TWO

The Americans

10.

A HORSELESS COMMANDER

In 1942, Alois Podhajsky was building up the Spanish Riding School in Vienna, and Gustav Rau was expanding his Nazi horse empire in Poland. The Nazi occupation of Europe was still successfully expanding. All the while, in the United States, the U.S. Army Remount Service (the U.S. counterpart to Gustav Rau's horse-breeding operations) was increasing breeding and acquisition of warhorses. These horses were being prepared to enter the European war.

Each part of the armed forces had its specialized job, and in 1941, the United States Cavalry's job was horses. At Fort Riley, the army's premier equestrian training center, a hundred-thousand-acre complex in the Flint Hills of northeastern Kansas, an increasing urgency filled the air. Ace equestrian Major Hank Reed and his men were training hard for a war that seemed more and more likely. Just three years earlier, Reed had crossed paths with Gustav Rau during the Reich equestrians' visit to Fort Leavenworth.

Hank Reed had spent a third of all his waking hours on horseback. Reed was the best of the best. He was born on a gentleman's farm near Richmond, Virginia, son of a wealthy textile merchant. He moved easily in the army's high society, but he was equally at home—probably more so—on a dusty parade field. His eyes were accustomed to looking out over vast distances at a gallop, the wind rushing past, whispering that the world was full of possibilities. Hank and his wife, Janice, had no children, which made him only more devoted to his animals, his horses, and, most of all, his men.

Everything that mattered in Hank Reed's life, outside of his family, revolved around horses. The rhythm of a horse's strides was like music to him. He walked, talked, moved, and stood still like a cavalryman. This was an art, and Hank Reed, age forty-one, was master of it. The only problem was that it was a dying art.

When Reed entered West Point in 1918, the First World War had just come to an end. That war definitively proved that horses were no match for the modern technology of war: machine guns, airpower, and chemical warfare. But still, on the banks of the Hudson River, the cadets spent hours on the parade grounds, mastering the skills of mounted combat that recent history had already shown were outdated. The War Department continued to support its mounted force, skeptical that motorized vehicles would be as mobile as horses. Besides, the cavalry had a rich ceremonial and sporting tradition that seemed worth preserving.

Throughout the 1920s and 1930s, the army cavalry had been immersed in an argument about what to do with the horses: One group, the die-hard horse folk, argued that the cavalry and the horse were inseparable. The other group insisted that the force's traditional tactics—surveillance, reconnaissance, and mobility—could just as easily be achieved using cars and tanks instead of horses. In the year 1940, the United States produced 4,280,000 cars. The transition from horsepower to motorized vehicles was increasingly thought to be the wave of the future.

The wire from the War Department summoning Hank Reed to a new command arrived a week shy of his forty-third birthday. One year after the Japanese attack on Pearl Harbor, the army was expanding fast: Reed had been promoted to lieutenant colonel, and for the first time, he would command an entire regiment. Before reporting to Fort Jackson, South Carolina, he was spending Christmas with his family in Richmond, Virginia. For Reed the horseman, this trip had a melancholy edge. Until now, he had always traveled with his horses, moving them from base to base. With the frenzy of preparations for war, this was no longer possible. Reed had brought his two polo ponies, Tea Kettle and Skin Quarter, home to his family's farm in Richmond, where they would remain until the war was over. In the cozy stables, Reed went about his chores with ease as he settled the two horses down for the night. The two chestnuts followed Hank's movements with their big, soft eyes. The horses had traveled with him from his previous posts, but today Hank Reed was saying goodbye to his horses for a long while. As he stroked their velvety noses and spoke a few soft words to each, he did not know when he would see them again.

As the new year of 1943 was rung in, all over America, young men and seasoned ones alike, in big cities and small towns, from

Arizona to Maine, bade farewell to wives and sweethearts, children and grandparents. During 1942, 3.9 million Americans were enlisted in the armed services. By the end of 1943, that number would swell to 9.1 million.

Just after the New Year, Lieutenant Colonel Reed shipped out for Fort Jackson, joining the throng of uniformed men jamming railcars all over the country. Like most of these men, Reed would arrive at a camp that had the ramshackle look of a work in progress: Crews were busy throwing together barracks, building mess halls, and preparing for the arrival of new soldiers. Reed's regiment was just starting. So far, only a small group of officers formed a nucleus. The small group would grow a regiment from the ground up.

Just eight days later, at ten-thirty a.m. on January 15, 1943, Lieutenant Colonel Reed stepped up on a makeshift podium set in the middle of a grassy parade ground. Decked out in the cavalry's high boots and flared breeches, Reed looked handsome, his hair crisply parted in the middle. Today was the official reactivation of the 2nd Cavalry, one of the army's most celebrated cavalry regiments, which had won glory in some of the most decisive mounted battles of the last century. Today was both a rebirth and a rechristening, Reed declared. From this day forward, the new 2nd Cavalry would have the word *mechanized* added to its name.

As he spoke, Hank felt the mantle of responsibility firmly settle on his shoulders. These men would look to the lieutenant colonel to be everything—father figure, mayor, judge, minister, and physician. He would mediate disputes and mete out punishment; he would provide for material and spiritual needs. For the foreseeable future, Hank Reed, whose hands were accustomed to gripping leather reins, a polo mallet, or a riding crop, would hold something infinitely more precious: the destiny of the men he had been entrusted to lead, and the fears, hopes, and prayers of the loved ones who were left behind.

By January 22, the new recruits started to pour onto the base. Some young men wore double-breasted suits and felt fedoras, sent off by their families in their Sunday best. But often the suits were threadbare and carefully mended. They were suits for farm boys whose parents still felt the pinch from the decade of the Great Depression. Their clothes were dusty, their shoes scuffed, and most carried a single battered leather valise, just large enough for a few personal possessions. They fell into line behind a sergeant and marched out of the train station, beginning to feel how different their lives were soon to become.

One of these young men, seventeen-year-old Jim O'Leary of Chicago, soon caught Hank Reed's eye. The young Irishman had a tousled mop of dark hair and a face that was all smile. While some of the other recruits were grumpy or shy, O'Leary seemed to know everyone by name and had a friendly word for all of them. The new recruit had lost his father at a young age and later rebuilt his mother's house with his own hands after it burned to the ground. Reed tapped O'Leary to be his personal driver. Everyone in the 2nd Cavalry saw Lieutenant Colonel Reed as a father figure, but between O'Leary and Reed there was a special affection—the fatherless boy was determined to look out for his commander from that moment on.

✦ ✦ ✦

The streets of Columbia, South Carolina, twelve miles west of Fort Jackson, were filled with soldiers. They all knew that they were teetering on a high wire—out there was the war, and that was where all of the young men were headed.

Among this mass of soldiers, clad in his neatly pressed army uniform and peaked cap, First Lieutenant Tom Stewart stood out for his well-mannered reserve. He was a bit older than some of the other new recruits, already a law school graduate. Dark-haired, not tall but well put together, he looked strong, though he bore his strength with a gentle manner. While he was prepared to do his duty for his country, Tom Stewart was more a lover than a fighter.

As the son of a prominent senator, Tom was a young man of privilege. But World War II was a time in the United States when servicemen enlisted from every walk of life, rich or poor, even the sons of senators. Tom was assigned to Lieutenant Colonel Reed's headquarters troop as an intelligence officer and would soon become someone his commander could count on for important tasks. But in January 1943, Tom was a new officer, following orders and trying to learn his job.

As time passed, this scraggly group of recruits lost their newness. Their days were filled with athletics, training on strategy, and long hikes. Their fitness improved, their bodies got harder, and the men learned to pull together as a team. On May 25, 1943, it was humid and raining and the roads were muddy and boggy when the men set out on their first hundred-mile hike. Sweaty, blistered, grimy, and undaunted, the men of the 2nd Cavalry had turned into soldiers. For the next nine months, the men continued to train and participate in maneuvers until all traces of their inexperience had been replaced by an easy sense of teamwork.

For a while, it had seemed as if the training would last forever, but on March 9, 1944, Hank Reed received an official letter from the War Department. The 2nd Cavalry Group was shipping out.

11.

AMERICA'S FIGHTIN'EST GENERAL

Bewdley, England, May 31, 1944

In May 1944, the number of Allied troops in England was growing by the day. Millions of soldiers needed to be supplied with uniforms, weapons, ammunition, food, and medical supplies. All of this man and machine power—including jeeps, planes, tanks, and artillery—would have to be carried across the water to mainland Europe. In the words of Dwight D. Eisenhower, it seemed as if the entire United Kingdom had been transformed into a giant military base. In Berlin, Hitler was aware of this massive influx of Allied forces, and had begun building a large-scale military construction along the coast of northwestern Europe. The only question was where and when the Allies would strike it.

At this time, the men in Janów Podlaski, Poland, were preparing to flee with the Arabians. The last fifteen white stallions of Vienna were putting on their last wartime performance before escaping to the countryside. And Colonel Reed and his men were gathering at Camp Bewdley in Britain's West Midlands, awaiting a visit from the commanding general of the Third Army.

A restless crowd of more than three thousand American soldiers waited for the big moment. The tall trees lining the roads into Camp Bewdley were swaying in a gentle breeze. The air was bright and fresh, and on a field facing the camp, a farmer and his horse tilled the soil, row after row. Atop a nearby hill, a group of local boys gathered, waiting to see the show.

Hank Reed, now a full colonel, sat on a platform with a dozen other XII Corps commanders watching long columns of troops march down the hill by company. This was the first time that the entire camp had been gathered altogether. The young soldiers were still unused to being so far from home. Most had arrived only weeks or days before. But today, they marched with a distinct sense of purpose.

After a few minutes, the bright sound of brass horns filled the air when a band seated next to the waiting speaker's platform began to play an upbeat march. The PA system crackled as a captain stepped up to the microphone and said, "When the general arrives, the band will play the General's March, and you will all stand."

A moment later, a soldier stationed near the road turned and started to wave as a long black car, blindingly shiny in the bright sunlight, zoomed up the road.

The door to the black car swung open, and out stepped General George S. Patton. Resplendent in high, brown cavalry field boots and a gleaming helmet, he walked briskly down the hillside toward the ten-man guard of honor, who stood at attention. Patton passed slowly in front of them, looking each soldier up and down and then peering into each one's face. From there, he walked straight up onto the platform.

Most of these soldiers were awestruck, having never seen the famous commander in person. This was not the case for Patton's fellow cavalryman Hank Reed, who had been acquainted with him for many years. Though Patton was eighteen years Reed's senior, the two officers shared a strong tie. Each had been a member of the prestigious War Department polo team, Patton in the 1920s and Reed in the 1930s. Since the invasion of North Africa and Sicily, in which the general had played a starring role, George Patton's name had been familiar in every American household. But Reed had known him as a rough-and-tumble polo player possessed of a foul mouth and a fierce competitive spirit.

Patton, like many others in the army, had believed that during peacetime, when soldiers weren't in combat, the horseback battles played on the polo field were the best way to train a man for combat. If Patton's theory was right, then the ace polo player Hank Reed was among the best-prepared soldiers at Camp Bewdley that day. None of the 2nd Cavalry men had seen real combat before, including their leader, Colonel Reed.

The general approached the microphone and looked out over the great mass of soldiers standing at attention on the hillside. "Be seated," he said. His amplified voice echoed out across the hillside, high and clear. His tone was firm and commanding. In a rolling wave, the men sank back down onto the grass.

"Men, this stuff we hear about America wanting to stay out of the war, not wanting to fight? Americans love to fight—traditionally. All real Americans love the sting and clash of battle. When you were kids you all admired the champion marble player, the fastest runner, the big-league ball players, the toughest boxers. Americans love a winner and will not tolerate a loser. Americans play to win—all the time . . ."

Up on the hillside, the men of the 2nd Cavalry listened intently. All of them knew that General Patton was the one who got called in when the going got tough. Indeed, the general then told the crowd that his presence in Bewdley was to be kept strictly top secret. Nobody knew exactly what was coming next; they just knew that they would be part of something bigger than all of them.

From where Patton stood, up on the platform, the Third Army looked like an enormous sea of men gathered with a common purpose. Despite the uniforms that made them resemble one another, every soldier sitting there that day had his own life story, his own pathway that had brought him to that place. Hank Reed himself had had twenty years to prepare for this moment.

"You are not going to die," Patton insisted. "Only two percent of you here, in a major battle, would die. Death must not be feared. Every man is frightened at first in battle. If he says he isn't, he's a . . . liar." Every man on that hillside was asking himself the same question: How would he react when his moment came? Not just would he be killed, but, more important, would he be brave enough? Here on the hillside, it was all narrowing down to the essence: one group, one task, and one goal.

Finally, Patton paused and, gripping the microphone, cast his gaze out over the assembled men. By the end of his rousing speech, he'd cracked plenty of jokes and the sounds of guffawing, thigh slapping, and cheers rang up from the assembled soldiers. "Old Blood and Guts" had scored well with the men.

Just six days later, on June 6, 1944—D-Day—the invasion of France began. The men of the 2nd Cavalry were surprised by the magnitude of the operation when they saw the skies jammed with fighters and bombers heading for the south coast of England and on to France. That day, each soldier understood that his training was about to be put to the test. But the cavalrymen had little time for reflection as they waited their turn to ship out for France. The next six weeks were a frenzy of preparation and movement: The 2nd Cavalry underwent introduction to new kinds of weapons, built and memorized relief maps, helped unload wounded German prisoners, and took classes in French and German.

Then they got their marching orders. They were headed for the Continent: the battleground of the war.

On the morning of July 16, the young men caught their first views of the gray waters of the English Channel. At five a.m., their convoy set sail. The convoy's thirty-one ships made a stately procession across the Channel, escorted by U.S. Navy destroyers and corvettes. From time to time, they passed through ghostly banks of fog, but mostly, the sea was calm. The ship's atmosphere was jittery, a heady mixture of dread and anticipation. The men ate and drank heartily, not knowing when they would see their next hot meal.

England was at their backs; in front of them stretched the continent of Europe. Somewhere, thousands of miles away, their families were home. Meanwhile, they were stepping boldly toward an uncertain future, driven by their senses of duty, honor, and courage.

12.

TWO HANDS AND A PURPLE HEART

Lunéville, France, September 18, 1944

In the autumn of 1944, as Alois Podhajsky was struggling to decide whether he should evacuate the remaining Lipizzaners from the Spanish Riding School in Vienna, Hank Reed and his men were fighting their way across the Aube region of northeastern France.

For the average soldier in Reed's 2nd Cavalry, the combat experience was made up of long stretches of boredom and discomfort, interrupted by fiery bursts of action. Tension was their constant companion—that and the mud clogging their vehicle tires, and the canned meat and cheese, crackers, and malted milk balls from their K rations, the ready-made meals supplied to the soldiers. Consistently operating behind enemy lines, they were dubbed "the ghosts" by the German forces because they often seemed to materialize out of nowhere. By late August, they had traveled close to three hundred hard-fought miles since landing on the beaches of Normandy.

From the perspective of the cavalrymen under Reed's

command, the war was fought step by step. Each hillock and river crossing was its own challenge, and so was each bridge and fork in the road. As commander of the entire 2nd Cavalry Group, with its two main units, the 42nd and 2nd squadrons, Hank Reed had the job of seeing the bigger picture. All together, more than four hundred men were under his command. Each squadron had six troops, lettered A through F, and each of these troops was made up of about twenty soldiers, along with tanks, guns, armored cars, half-tracks, and jeeps. In addition, Reed traveled with the Headquarters Troop, which included intelligence, medical, and supply officers. A group of specialized interrogators also moved with the 2nd.

The American cavalry rumbled across France on country lanes where some days the mud was as formidable a foe as the enemy guns. Though Reed's "horses" were powered by gasoline instead of hay, the philosophy that drove their mission was unchanged from their mounted days. The American cavalry was fully mechanized—meaning they used motorized vehicles instead of horses. Not so the Germans. Reed and his men had to face the reality of aiming their weapons at men on horses on the field of battle, and as they crossed France on their four-wheeled stallions, they sometimes witnessed or were involved in situations when horses were brutally caught in the cross fire.

As the Third Army maintained a breakneck pace while moving east across France, Reed's command post moved frequently, keeping up with their position at the vanguard of the American front. Between August and September 1944, he moved forty times. Between camps, Reed led his command from a jeep strategically positioned in a gully or grove. Always in danger of a surprise encounter with the enemy, Sergeant Jim O'Leary drove swiftly. Usually, Reed relocated either early in the morning or in the late afternoon, first sending out an advanced squad to select the site. It was not uncommon to move twice in one day.

The dangers of war were not foreign to these soldiers. Recently, Reed had lost one of his best men, Major Jim Pitman. Reed had had tremendous faith in the young major's leadership and courage. The major had been a man he could count on. The two had served together since the beginning, at Fort Jackson. With a heavy heart, Reed could picture Pitman's bright blue eyes peering out from under his helmet. Hank Reed frequently found himself in the cross fire of danger, too. One particularly explosive experience ended with his being sent to Paris for surgery on his right hand. He would recover, but he would never regain full use of that hand. His polo-playing days were behind him. Yet, when visitors came to see him at the hospital, Reed said nothing at all about himself. He just asked after his men, in particular wanting to know how the other wounded cavalrymen were doing. Forever after, Reed would carry in his mind the shadow of the fallen men in his command.

By December 1944, he was back with his men in Luxembourg. Colonel Reed would celebrate his forty-fourth birthday, December 25, back holding the reins of the 2nd Cavalry.

From Third Army Headquarters came General Patton's greeting:

> To each officer and soldier in the Third United States Army, I wish a Merry Christmas. I have full confidence in your courage, devotion to duty, and skill in battle. We march in our might to complete victory. May God's blessings rest upon each of you on this Christmas Day.

On that Christmas Day, all was quiet as drifts of snow piled up around their tents and road-scarred vehicles. The day passed mostly peacefully while the men enjoyed their Red Cross Yule packages and letters from their loved ones.

Back at their home in Virginia, Reed's wife, Janice, and their family gathered around the large mahogany table. Down at the barn, Tea Kettle and Skin Quarter gazed out over winter-brown fields whitened with frost, stamping their feet as their nostrils made plumes of white steam in the air. In homes all over America, holiday tables were set with one less place.

Reed and his men, camped in the bleak midwinter, must have wondered right then what their purpose was—but the 2nd Cavalry's greatest days were still to come. As they continued on their way east, the winter would thaw, and the Germans would get pushed back. By April 1945, Reed's 2nd Cavalry would have covered more territory, killed more enemy soldiers, captured more prisoners, and suffered fewer casualties than any other regiment of comparable size stationed in Europe. The snow would melt, the Germans would fight their last battles, and the 2nd Cavalry would be offered the chance to embark on their most exhilarating adventure.

But right now, Christmas 1944, they were grateful to pass a silent night.

PART THREE

The Mission

13.

ARMIES CLOSING IN

Bohemia, Czechoslovakia, Late April 1945

Four months had passed since the bleak Christmas of 1944. By April of 1945, massive Russian and American forces marched toward each other from east and west, the gap between them shrinking every day. Between these two fronts, Germany was crumbling. Trapped, millions of refugees were trying to flee to safer areas. In the chaos of the Third Reich's near collapse, the displaced Lipizzaners were in great danger.

Along a country lane, near the village of St. Martin in Upper Austria, Alois Podhajsky sat astride Neapolitano Africa, eyes trained on his horse's sensitive ears. Podhajsky was engaged in a wordless conversation with his mount. His seat, legs, and reins picked up clues to his horse's emotions. Podhajsky's face was serene, and his posture in the saddle appeared just as erect as it had nine years earlier, when he had ridden across the stadium at the Olympics in Berlin. He rapidly scanned the woods that lined the road, then glanced back at Africa's tapered white ears.

Sometimes his horse heard the approach of the dive bombers before his own ears could pick up the sound.

Africa's ear flicked twice, and Podhajsky felt the stallion tense slightly underneath him. Podhajsky raised his hand, signaling his fellow riders to take shelter with him under a small thicket of trees, though the horses, with their bright white coats, would be easily visible from the air.

Overhead, the drone of an airplane became audible, buzzing more and more loudly until it seemed to hang directly overhead, then fading to a rasp in the distance. No one said a word. When the danger had passed, Podhajsky rode back into the open. The other riders silently followed. Each time this happened, Podhajsky questioned the safety of exercising the stallions out in the open. But what choice did he have?

Podhajsky and his riders were lodged in the Arco Castle in St. Martin, where they had taken refuge after fleeing Vienna. They were not the castle's only inhabitants; it was packed with other German refugees who had fled the Reich's eastern territories. Their rooms in the former servants' wing were humble, but Podhajsky knew that they were fortunate. The village was full to the bursting point with Russian and Polish prisoners of war who had been brought in to work on the local farms. They were restless and volatile, waiting for the war's end to bring their liberation. This small town was shadowed by despair and anger.

Podhajsky understood that to these suffering people, the fate of the white stallions was unimportant. Some of the refugees said aloud that they didn't care about the horses. Many even thought they should be slaughtered to add to the meager food supply.

Foremost in everyone's mind was the fear of *which* occupying force would arrive first. Would it be the Russians, who by this time had already seized Vienna? Or would it be the Americans, who were fanning out across Germany and were less than a hundred miles away?

One day late that April, Podhajsky was surprised to find a visitor who had come all the way from Berlin to visit the horses. It was General Erich Weingart, chief of riding and driving in the German Army's High Command, the same individual who had given Podhajsky permission to evacuate the stallions from Vienna if the Nazis agreed.

The general walked through the stables slowly, stopping to look at each of the horses in turn. As the two men walked in the gardens before dinner, Podhajsky confided his fears: His riders, during German occupation, had worn the Wehrmacht uniform. He was afraid that if the Russians arrived, these men would be seized as prisoners of war. Already, each rider was responsible for ten horses. If the riders were taken away, who would be left to guard them? But the general reassured him; the Americans would arrive in their area before the Russians, he said. "You will succeed in putting these soldiers as deeply under the spell of your white horses as you have always managed to do with me."

General Weingart continued, "I will have a document drawn up for you, duly signed and sealed and to be put into immediate effect, removing the Spanish Riding School from the command of the army and declaring it once more a civil riding school as it was before 1938. Perhaps this document may help you cope with the transition period more easily. For me, this final service to the Spanish Riding School will be the last good deed of my life."

The general parted emotionally with Podhajsky that day. Podhajsky couldn't believe his good fortune. Soon his beloved school would be under Austrian rule—no longer in Nazi control.

Less than a week later, the sound of artillery fire could be heard in the distance, heralding the Americans' approach.

Grimly, Podhajsky realized that whatever happened next would be unpredictable and dangerous. Trying not to draw attention to himself, he began to prepare for the end: He hid some of their most valuable equipment behind a bricked-up partition inside the castle and stashed away civilian clothes so that his riders might not be noticed among the other refugees. The last thing he wanted was for these riders to be taken as prisoners of war. He knew that everything he had done so far to safeguard the horses could easily be swept away in these final days of conflict.

The riders took turns standing at the stables. They were keeping guard. It was hard to tell how many people remained loyal to the Nazis and would put up a fight. If the Nazi hold-outs chose to fight when the American tanks arrived, the animals might be caught in the cross fire. On the other hand, if Podhajsky and his riders avoided fighting and appeared eager to surrender to the Americans, the Nazis might shoot them for being "traitors."

As their tense wait continued, Podhajsky carefully rationed the remaining grain: He had been getting extra feed from Hostau, but recently, that had stopped. He received nothing—neither feed nor word of the mares and foals. He feared the worst.

✦ ✦ ✦

About a hundred miles south of St. Martin lay the stud farm at Hostau. The farm appeared eerily untouched by the ravages of war. In the well-kept stallion barn, Witez, plump and sleek, peered over the half door of his stall. His warm, throaty whinny greeted the veterinarian Rudolf Lessing, who was hurrying through the stables. Late April was foaling season, and most of Lessing's attention was focused on the broodmares.

In the long barn with the wide foaling stalls, Lessing quietly observed the mares, noting which ones would give birth soon. Having for years spent most of his waking hours among horses, he could read their thoughts and understand their expressions. Sometimes when he saw the trusting way they responded to him, especially the mares, heavily pregnant or with newborns by their sides, his heart ached. The horses were at their most defenseless during foaling season. Even here in Bohemia, one of the most sheltered places to ride out the war, no one could ignore the melancholy atmosphere lurking below the surface calm. Lessing kept his mind on the work at hand, but the looming danger of war was never far from his thoughts.

By now, Hostau was cut off from the German Reich due to a breakdown in communications. News arrived at Hostau in panicked rumors and whispers. The official German radio still reported the triumph of Hitler's Reich. But late at night, as Lessing and his wife leaned toward a secret radio tuned to an Allied station, he learned the truth: The tide of war had turned against the Nazis. The Russians were advancing rapidly west. Like many of his countrymen, Lessing believed that the war would end soon in German defeat. As clear as this was, for anyone to even *express* such a thought out loud was punishable as treason by the Nazis.

German-speaking civilians, fleeing from intense fighting farther east, began pouring into town. They were fearful that the Russians and Czechs would show no mercy at the end of the war, and so were trying to make it across the border into Germany. A few lucky ones had cars or trucks; most had overloaded wagons pulled by worn-out horses; the most pitiful walked, carrying bundles or young children in their arms. The veterinarian lent a hand whenever he could to help the worn-out and wounded animals.

Even here on the stud farm, the pastures were now teeming with extra stock. In mid-March 1945, one of Rau's stud farm directors had straggled into town, accompanied by a Russian duke seeking shelter for his herd of sturdy Kabardins and rugged Panje ponies, bred on the Russian steppes. They had fled nearly four hundred miles, from one of the stud farms run by Gustav Rau in central Poland, to find refuge in Hostau. Lessing knew that this group was better prepared than other fleeing horsemen—the Cossack horses were bred to be hardy and to subsist on sparse rations, and the Cossack equestrians were skilled outriders who knew how to herd horses over long distances. Lessing and his colleagues could only imagine the fates of the horses that hadn't made it out of the eastern part of Rau's empire, but he suspected that many of them were scattered— even dead.

The farm had also completely lost touch with Alois Podhajsky and the white stallions of Vienna. None of them knew if the historic riding school was still standing. Lessing feared for himself, for his family, and most of all for the swollen-bellied mares and tiny newborn foals who trusted him to keep them safe.

✦ ✦ ✦

Colonel Hubert Rudofsky still ran Hostau for Rau, and his tall leather boots, polished to a high shine, clicked across the cobblestone floors at Hostau as he scanned the stables with an exacting eye. Next to Rudofsky stood Hostau's latest visitor: German air force colonel Walter Hölters. Hölters was roughly the same age as Rudofsky, around fifty, and about half a head shorter. Just above his tightly closed lips, he sported a narrow Hitler-style mustache.

It was unclear what the visiting colonel was there for, but Rudofsky agreeably toured him around the farm. With enthusiasm, Rudofsky gave special attention to the gray Arabian Lotnik, one of the imports from Janów—and a favorite stallion of Rau's. With pride, he pointed out the stallion's exceptional characteristics: luminous dark eyes, clean straight legs, and exquisitely fine fluted nostrils. Hölters listened attentively to Rudofsky, aware that the stud farm master of Hostau was known to be one of the Reich's foremost horse-breeding experts. One thing was certain: Rudofsky had sensed that this man's enthusiasm for the horses was real; his knowledge about the Lipizzaners and the Spanish Riding School seemed authentic to the core.

Hölters had not explained to Rudofsky exactly what his business was in the area. He had found that sticking to horse talk was a lot safer than discussing politics. But when the tour was over, the visitor signaled that he wished to speak to Rudofsky privately. As the two men strolled toward the pastures, out of earshot of curious grooms, the officer whispered to Rudofsky that he had important information to share. "Vienna has already fallen to the Russians," he said. "The Red Army is just

outside Pilsen, less than forty miles away. They will be here before you know it."

Rudofsky absorbed this news with shock. Pilsen was the
nearest large town to the east; if what the officer said was true,
the Russian conquerors would be upon them in a matter of
days—possibly even hours.

"I've spent time on the Eastern Front," Hölters continued.
"The Russians care nothing for horses—they will slaughter
them on the spot and fry them up as steaks to feed their hungry
troops. You are in the greatest danger, and you must act now to
save them."

At these shocking words, Rudofsky flinched. He scrutinized the officer's face. What solution could this man possibly
suggest that he himself hadn't already thought of and ruled out?
For one thing, he'd received a direct order to remain at Hostau.
Just a week before, he had contacted Berlin, asking what to do if
the stud farm was in danger of being overrun. He received only
the curt reply: "Stay put, at all costs." But even if Rudofsky were
allowed to move the horses, it would be practically impossible.
It was the middle of foaling season. They had neither trucks to
transport the horses nor gasoline. Until now, Hostau *itself* had
been the refuge. Where could be safer than here?

Rudofsky listened intently to Hölters, desperately hop-
ing that this officer could suggest a better solution. But what
Hölters said next shook him. "You must make contact with the
Americans. They are not far—just over the border to Bavaria.
Perhaps you can deliver the horses to them. It's your only hope."

The Americans? Rudofsky was shocked to the core. This officer, a stranger to him, was suggesting what Rudofsky had not
imagined in his wildest dreams. It was unthinkable, ridiculous,

it bordered on the insane. He was advising Rudofsky to make contact with the enemy, an act of high treason! Rudofsky silently ticked through the possibilities. Perhaps the officer had been sent specifically to test his loyalties, laying out a trap for him to stumble into. Even more terrifying, perhaps he spoke the truth. If their best hope was to surrender to the Americans, then clearly, they had run out of options.

After instructing Rudofsky to await further communication, Hölters got back into his car and drove away.

Of all the horsemen in the Reich, Rudofsky had been selected to be in charge of these Arabians and Lipizzaner, their most precious horses. Now, if he spent too long thinking about how to keep them safe, it would be too late to act. Catastrophe was imminent, but Rudofsky remained deeply uncertain whether he should take the colonel's advice. What would the Americans do if he approached them?

Horses had been here before Hitler's Third Reich arrived, and horses would be here, Rudofsky believed, after Hitler was gone. He was reluctant to flee with the horses—not because he didn't care about their well-being. Nothing was more important to him. But where, he wondered, could he protect them better than here in Hostau, where he was a highly respected member of the community? The safest thing for the horses, in Rudofsky's opinion, was for them to remain at the farm.

Weary and battle-worn, Hank Reed and the 2nd Cavalry had been fighting their way eastward since Christmas 1944.

Everyone was predicting German defeat any day. But even so, as they marched closer to the end of the war, Reed was losing men from his ranks almost daily. It was always painful to lose a man, but somehow, the closer the end seemed, the more each loss hurt. He could see the prospect of home flickering in the back of each man's mind, even his own. He had to try not to think about the mothers and sweethearts at home—the ones reading in the newspapers that the war was almost over, the ones who were allowing themselves to believe that surely their loved one would make it home.

They had pushed so far into Germany that the Czechoslovakian border was just a few kilometers away. Just over that border, unbeknownst to them, lay the still-peaceful village of Hostau.

The late-April sun shone down on all of them:

On Podhajsky, who knew that the next few days would most likely decide his stallions' fate.

On Lessing, who nursed the mares and foals, wondering what would become of them.

On Rudofsky, a man who had been thrust unwillingly into the most momentous decision of his life.

And on Hank Reed, a man who loved horses, who had no idea he was about to be given the chance of a lifetime.

The sun also shone upon the horses—reflecting glints of sunlight on the backs of the white stallions in St. Martin, and the broodmares in Hostau, and Witez's blood bay coat, which shone like burnished bronze.

The next few days would determine the fate of all of them, humans and horses alike.

14.

THE PHOTOGRAPHS

Near the Czechoslovakian Border, April 25, 1945

Hank Reed stood inside a rustic farmhouse in a village in southern Germany. Peering out the window, he could see pock-marked buildings with caved-in walls. American tanks had destroyed them a few days earlier.

Reed had just received an important report. Slowly, he took in all of its layers: A German intelligence group had recently fled Berlin, desperate to escape before the Russians took over the capital. Now they were holed up in a place called Diana-hof, a hunting lodge in the Bohemian Forest. This forest was so deeply wooded that the trees created a thick natural barrier. The men, made up of high-ranking officers, were calling themselves a "meteorological group" to hide their spy activities. They were believed to be transporting highly secret photographs and maps documenting the location of Russian airfields and industry. That was all he knew. Reed's commander at XII Corps headquarters made it clear that the capture of this group—and those documents—was a high-priority mission.

Reed summoned Captain Ferdinand Sperl, a valuable interrogator of prisoners of war. Sperl, who was born in Switzer-
land, was fluent in German and knew the local area. Behind
his fun-loving demeanor, he was also highly intelligent and a
skilled linguist. Reed relied on him to handle missions requir-
ing sophisticated language skills and diplomatic tact.

When Sperl came to greet him at headquarters, Reed had
a map spread out on the table. He showed Sperl a location just
over the Czechoslovakian border, a few miles away—the hunting lodge called Dianahof.

"There are about twenty men hiding up there, fleeing Berlin," Reed explained. "We need to capture them and, most importantly, keep their documents intact."

It was a dangerous mission.

Figure it out, Reed told Sperl. Sperl named the mission Operation Sauerkraut.

The next afternoon, before Sperl had finished making his
plans, a car slowly approached a 2nd Cavalry headquarters
checkpoint with a white flag fluttering from its antenna—a
symbol that meant "I come in peace." The American soldiers
peered curiously at the car. Inside they saw an officer of the
German air force. He was middle-aged, short, and had a narrow mustache that somewhat resembled Hitler's.

The German demanded an interview with Colonel Harry
Reed, claiming that he had "urgent information." Sperl swiftly
intercepted. Nobody got to Colonel Reed without speaking to
him first.

"Come with me," Sperl said, masking his curiosity. He escorted the visitor to his interrogation tent, looking him over
with a practiced eye. *Who was this German coming in peace?*

Sperl was born people-smart, and his training as an interrogator had only sharpened his skills. He noted the German's distinctive small mustache and the pince-nez glasses, which gave
him a scholarly look.

Sperl gestured for the man to be seated. "What brings you
here?" he asked. Sperl's German was Swiss-accented, but his
demeanor had a friendly swagger that was one hundred percent
American.

"I come here on urgent business," the officer replied. "I need
to speak with the commanding officer."

Sperl's face was open, and though his expression was mild, it
was clear that he meant business. He started with simple questions. "Name and rank?"

"Colonel Walter H.," the German replied. "I need to speak
to the commanding officer."

Sperl was familiar with this tactic. Intelligence officers who
were negotiating refused to give their last names. He flipped
open the officer's seized wallet, looking for clues to his identity.
The officer had removed all identification cards. But the wallet
was not entirely empty. Sperl saw the serrated edges of some
photographs and slid them out. He was expecting well-worn
pictures of wives or children. Sometimes these keepsakes offered clues to their bearer's identity.

Sperl was surprised. Instead of family members, he was
looking at two photographs of beautiful, glowing white horses.
The officer watched the American expectantly; Sperl could tell
right away that these pictures mattered a lot to him. Now it was
his job to learn *why*.

"Why do you have these pictures?" Sperl asked. He made an
effort to keep his tone friendly and patient.

The officer hesitated, obviously weighing whether he should tell his tale to the captain. "I took these photographs just a few days ago. Not far from here, in a village called Hostau, there is an old imperial horse-breeding station . . ."

Sperl nodded for the man to go on.

"In this location, some of the most valuable horses in the world are being sheltered."

Sperl eyed the officer carefully. "Did you come here from Hostau? Is that where you are stationed?"

"No," the officer replied.

"Why are you concerning yourself with this matter?"

A half smile crossed the colonel's face. "I'm a lover of horses," he said.

"So, you are not stationed at Hostau, but you are a horse fancier . . ." Sperl leaned in, peering at the officer's face. "And who are you, *exactly?*"

The officer's answer was clearly well rehearsed. "I'm a meteorologist, part of a meteorological group recently evacuated from Berlin."

A meteorological group recently evacuated from Berlin? A bell rang in Sperl's head. Colonel H. *must* be a spy. And not just any spy—one of the exact spies he was looking for.

Sperl looked straight into the officer's eyes. "You're not telling the truth," Sperl said calmly. "You're not a meteorologist. You're part of an intelligence group. You're staying at a hunting lodge called Dianahof not far from here. You were fleeing Berlin when you ran out of gas."

The colonel's eyes widened in surprise, but he betrayed no emotion. "I need to speak to your commanding officer," he repeated.

Sperl held firm. "Explain why you have pictures of horses."

The officer, perhaps realizing that he would not get to the commander if he did not cooperate, explained.

"These are no ordinary horses. They are royal Lipizzaners from Vienna. The German Army sent them to Hostau for safekeeping. Now they are in danger of being captured by the advancing Russian Army. I want to speak to your commanding officer to see if he can help."

Taking the two photographs, Sperl went looking for Colonel Reed. He had a hunch that his commanding officer, or CO, was going to find this new development very interesting indeed. The German colonel had no idea just how lucky he was. Of all the American army commanders in Europe, only a handful were passionate horsemen. Hank Reed had arrived in Europe at the head of a horseless cavalry, but when it came time to choose the code name for his regiment, he came up with one that revealed what was deep in his heart: Thoroughbred. When Sperl showed Reed the two photographs, his CO reacted with utter surprise.

The last thing he expected to see out here was beautiful purebred horses. Since the war started, he'd seen enough sorry specimens to last him a lifetime—horses hitched to artillery wagons, half-starved horses pulling heavy loads, starving refugees eating exhausted horses. Reed scrutinized the photos before him. When a layman looks at a horse, he will see the obvious things like size and color, but when a horseman looks at a horse, a million tiny details catch his notice. Reed saw the snow-white animal's perfectly formed legs, a well-shaped face, and small, tapered ears. The horse's coat shone with good health like a brilliant pearl. His eyes peered soulfully toward the camera. Here was a specimen so rare that a uniformed German officer would come under a flag of peace to beg that it be saved.

Reed decided to play along—but he needed more information first. The Americans would do their best to bring the horses in Hostau to safety, he explained to the visitor, but only under certain conditions. He laid out his terms: The German intelligence group must surrender with all of their documents. If they met Reed's demands, they would be interrogated at the European Theater Operations headquarters. There, they would not be treated as prisoners of war. They would work with the Allies *only* in regard to their intelligence about Russia, which meant that they would not be committing treason.

The officer agreed with a crisp nod. He would bring Sperl to Dianahof under a white flag to arrange the terms of surrender. Reed asked about the documents. The German colonel explained that the group had maps and photographs buried in crates on the grounds of the lodge. Reed and Sperl exchanged a look of triumph when the German added that the hidden documents would fill an entire truck—this was a treasure of great scope. That is, if they were able to pull it off, and if this officer could be trusted.

At dusk, Sperl set off with the German officer toward Dianahof. The road wound upward through ever-deepening pine forests, and darkness fell over them like a thick wool blanket. Sperl pulled his overcoat tighter around him as the jeep bumped over the rutted country road. He kept an eye on Colonel "Walter H.," the man who was now his guide. The forest was mostly quiet until they came across a roadblock manned by German sentries. Guards pulled out their rifles and fired shots into the air, splitting the silence.

Sperl waited, rigid, as the colonel gave the passwords that would let them through. His safety, his life, was at the mercy of an enemy officer he'd first laid eyes on only earlier that day. After a long, tense moment, the guards let them pass.

When they arrived, it was almost dark. Inside Dianahof, Sperl came face to face with the spies who called themselves a "meteorological group": two dozen Luftwaffe officers—women and men—who knew that their war was coming to an end. Sperl looked at them carefully and, as clearly as possible, laid out Reed's terms.

After much deliberation, the colonel announced their decision: The Germans would surrender themselves and all of their documents to the Americans. The German officers were edgy. For them, surrendering could be fraught with risks. If an SS detachment, Hitler's loyal diehards, got wind of the plan, they would be accused of treason—or possibly even killed. The officers finally agreed to go along with Reed and the Americans' plan, but they had only one request: They wanted to stage a sham firefight to make it *look* as if they hadn't surrendered to the Americans voluntarily.

Sperl agreed. He instructed them to dig up the crates filled with the documents and have them ready to hand over in the morning. The Americans would return at dawn the next day. If the mission succeeded, it would be a huge achievement—to capture an entire high-ranking German intelligence group with all of its documents. Nobody had yet said a word about horses.

✦ ✦ ✦

Sperl hardly managed to sleep that night. As soon as dawn broke, he and his men headed out, lumbering back up the mountain road. The noise of their vehicles rumbling over the roads echoed through the trees, giving an enemy plenty of time to prepare an ambush. But before long, they reached the hunting lodge.

Reflecting in the slanting rays of dawn sunlight, Dianahof was imposing, with peaked slate roofs and rows of tall windows glinting like peering eyes. A statue of Diana, the goddess of hunting, gazed serenely over the group.

Dressed in full uniform, the German colonel formally surrendered to the Americans. The German officers gathered their stacks of wooden crates, each one filled with valuable classified documents. It was time to turn them over. Somberly, the colonel oversaw the loading of the German documents onto the American trucks. For the first time, he gave Sperl his real name: Walter Hölters.

When the documents were secured, the convoy headed down the hill toward the German border. As soon as Sperl was a safe distance away, he heard the American tank bombarding the now-empty Dianahof lodge, quickly followed by machine-gun chatter to create the impression of cross fire. Once the noise of the fake skirmish subsided, Sperl and his prisoners found themselves alone on the mountain road with only the sounds of their trucks and jeeps to break the silence. Sperl heaved a sigh of relief. He radioed ahead to Colonel Reed: *Prepare for the arrival of the captives.*

Back at headquarters, Reed invited Hölters to share a meal and asked him for more information about the horses. Where exactly were they located? Who was guarding them? How many were there? What breeds were they? How many people were on the staff?

Hank Reed and Walter Hölters were on opposite sides of this cruel war. All around them, brutality, chaos, and bloodshed ruled the day. Still, between them, there was a scrap of understanding tied to their mutual regard for horses.

One thing was certain—the German had a plan to help Reed safeguard the animals. All he had to do was put it into action. First, Hölters penned a note to Hubert Rudofsky, the chief of the stud farm at Hostau, whom he had met a few days earlier. Then Hölters sent his assistant off to bring the note to a forester's house that lay in the woods, about halfway between Hostau and the American lines. The forester would then carry the note the rest of the way to Rudofsky.

The message from Hölters did not mention the Americans but gave instructions to Rudofsky about how to contact him regarding a possible escape route for the Lipizzaners.

In turn, Reed told his sentries to be on the lookout for a German soldier crossing over enemy lines, wanting to talk about horses.

The plan was in place. Now there was nothing to do but wait.

15.

THE PLAN

Rudolf Lessing hurried toward Rudofsky's office, where he had been summoned. The call could mean anything—a sick horse, a problem with a pregnant mare, or any number of small health problems that could crop up with horses day to day. When the veternarian arrived, the commander's face was grave. In his hand, Rudofsky held a letter.

Lessing listened thoughtfully as he revealed the secret purpose of Hölters's recent visit to Hostau; the colonel had urged him to evacuate the horses. After much agonizing reflection, Rudofsky had decided he was right. Just now a messenger had brought a note from Hölters promising an escape route for the horses. There were only two caveats: The plan was secret—and dangerous.

"An escape route?" Lessing asked. "But how? When?" He was thinking about the broodmares, some nearly ready to foal, others with tiny offspring at their side. They shouldn't be going anywhere in that state. But the urgency on Rudofsky's face was unmistakable. They needed to take immediate action.

Hölters's plan required a few complicated steps. First, Lessing would ride horseback into the thick Bohemian Forest and locate a forester's house where he would make contact with Colonel Hölters. To avoid raising suspicion, Rudofsky would stay behind on the farm. Lessing would take along a groom riding a second horse in case he needed to bring back a negotiator from the American side. They could trust no one. A wrong word or action, no matter how innocent, could lead to the most serious consequences.

His head spinning with a million unanswered questions, Lessing nodded curtly in agreement and left immediately for the stables. In the close quarters of the stall, he spoke softly to his Thoroughbred former racehorse, Indigo—so named because his coat was so black it appeared almost blue. In more peaceful times, Indigo had been a frequent race winner. These days, he had a far humbler task: carrying the veterinarian to house calls at neighboring farms. Today was likely the most important ride of his life.

There was no time to waste. Lessing and the groom set off at a brisk trot. His heart beating loudly, Lessing rode as if in a hurry, his straight back inclined forward, his heels sunk down. Indigo stretched his nose out, his long strides quickly covering ground. Alongside him, in sharp contrast to his pitch-black companion, was a white Yugoslavian Lipizzaner stallion whose snow-white mane floated from his powerful arched crest.

As a veterinarian, Lessing had clocked many miles in the saddle on these lands, and he was at ease in the fields and

country lanes. But Lessing knew that this ride was different.
He was taking a great risk that might end badly. Trying not to
think about his wife and daughters, who did not know about
this mission, he willed himself to be brave.

The closer they got to the edge of the forest, the less Lessing's anxiety nagged at him. Taking action felt better than the
previous weeks of uncertainty and waiting, but while dark-
coated Indigo was swallowed up in the black shadows, the Lipizzaner at his side glowed like a pale moon. At last they came
to the designated forester's lodge deep in the woods. They approached cautiously.

The forester was at home. Lessing asked if he had seen the
German colonel. The forester explained that Colonel Hölters
had departed, and furthermore, he believed that he might be
in American captivity. The forester offered the use of his stables and his motorcycle should Lessing wish to proceed in his
search. Unprepared for this news, Lessing pondered his options. Perhaps the smartest choice was to turn around. But Rudofsky had told him to make contact with Colonel Hölters. If
he returned to Hostau empty-handed, then what? They had no
backup plan.

Lessing agreed to leave the horses with the groom in the forester's stable and to proceed on the forester's motorcycle. As he
swerved toward the American camp, the sound of the motorcycle's engine battered his ears like gunfire.

"Hands up!" American soldiers toting machine guns blocked
his path.

Lessing cut the motor and froze. Fear clouded his brain.

The American soldiers stared at him. They pointed their guns directly at his chest. Lessing tried to explain that he was a veterinarian from a nearby horse-breeding farm, but the GIs seemed unsurprised to find him there. He knew nothing of Americans except that they were enemies—and now he just might be their prisoner. Fear and wild thoughts started banging around his brain. He wasn't sure what this might mean for him—a prison camp? Worse? Lessing tried to remind himself that he was doing this for the sake of the horses.

The sentries signaled to him to climb aboard their jeep. Before he had time to reflect upon his situation, he was taken to regimental headquarters and was standing face-to-face with an American colonel. Lessing made a split-second decision. Even though he had not been expecting to meet American soldiers, why not press the horses' case to his captors? He figured he had nothing to lose.

Hank Reed rubbed his hands together. So far, the plan with Walter Hölters had worked. Here before Reed stood a young German veterinary officer from Hostau. Reed listened as the man described the nearby remount depot and the valuable horses hidden there.

"The horses are in danger," Lessing said. "That is why I've come."

Reed assured the young officer that he had a plan: The German staff of the stud farm needed to transport the horses over the border. From there, the Americans would ensure their safety.

Carefully, Lessing began to explain why the horses couldn't

leave the farm. It was foaling season. Many of the mares had recently given birth or were just about to. They couldn't travel that distance on such short notice; the mares and foals could never walk that far, and they didn't have enough men or trucks, not to mention gasoline, to ship the horses. Besides, there were several hundred horses at Hostau. How could they possibly escape without notice?

Lessing tried to be both calm and forceful as he explained what needed to be done instead: The American army needed to occupy Hostau. He looked Reed in the eye and added that he was certain that his commander, Colonel Rudofsky, would agree to surrender the depot. The veterinarian sounded more confident than he felt. Privately he knew that Colonel Rudofsky had made no such promise.

"Regardless of what you decide," Lessing added, "I do not have the authority to make this decision. Give me an American officer. The officer should come with me and speak with Colonel Rudofsky, my superior." Lessing mentioned the two horses in the forester's lodge and said that the American officer could ride back with him easily.

Reed listened. He knew something that Lessing did not. American troops were forbidden to advance past the border of Czechoslovakia, where Hostau was. In February, at the Yalta Conference, President Franklin Delano Roosevelt and British Prime Minister Winston Churchill had agreed with Joseph Stalin, leader of the Russian Communist Party, that everything east of the border with Germany proper would be considered under Russian control. For Reed, this meant that the horses might be tantalizingly close, but they were heartbreakingly out of reach.

Reed considered his options. Could he risk lives and man-power on a crazy mission to save a group of horses? If he sent an officer to negotiate, the man would have to sneak across the border right under the noses of the enemy. If the officer got caught, he'd have to keep the mission a secret—perhaps even under torture. Putting men at risk was never an easy decision. But abandoning the horses just didn't feel right to him. He could not easily forget the cavalry lesson instilled in him over twenty years: Horses should always be treated well.

The more Reed thought about it, the more he realized there was just one man in the army who might be crazy enough to agree to a scheme like this: the man who had said of the cavalry-man, "You must be: a horse master; a scholar; a high minded gentleman; a cold blooded hero; a hot blooded savage. At one and the same time, you must be a wise man and a fool." The man who might be just enough of a wise man and a fool to agree to this plan was Hank's old polo buddy and mentor: the com-mander in chief of the Third Army, General George S. Patton.

16.

DRESSED UP AS A PLENIPOTENTIARY

Colonel Reed knew that there was little time to waste. Only a matter of miles separated them from the rapidly advancing Russian front. If this mission to Hostau was going to succeed at all, it had to happen fast, before somebody besides Patton got wind of it and told them to knock it off.

Reed needed the right man to accompany Rudolf Lessing back to Hostau: someone who could ride horseback, someone smart, someone whom he trusted. And he knew just the man for the job: Tennessee-born Tom Stewart. Captain Tom Stewart was mild-mannered, with a calm, confident air. He could understand some German, so he wouldn't be completely lost. Most important, Stewart had grown up around horses in his native Tennessee. The young man could ride well.

When Stewart was summoned to meet with Reed, he did not ask why. He hurried off to report to headquarters, and arrived just in time to see Hank Reed and a sergeant getting out of the vehicle that held the colonel's radio. Stewart didn't know at the time that Reed had just received a message from General George Patton himself.

Inside headquarters stood several American officers, including Sperl, whose bravery that morning with the "capture" of Walter Hölters had started the whole chain of events. With them was a young German officer who was introduced as Rudolf Lessing. The German spoke passable English with a clipped accent. His manner was polite and formal, but he was clearly uncomfortable. When Stewart arrived, Lessing was talking about a place called Hostau, just on the other side of the border. It was home to a collection of horses like no other in the world, and their lives were in danger.

As Tom Stewart listened, he started making sense of why he'd been invited to this meeting. Colonel Reed had decided to help this veterinarian evacuate the horses to a safer location. This German officer was an emissary from the stud farm who had come to try to negotiate terms. That was where Stewart would come in: He was going to ride with Lessing behind enemy lines—and when Colonel Reed said "ride," he meant on horseback. The object was to negotiate the peaceful surrender of the horse depot to the American army.

After three years in the cavalry, Stewart was an old hand, but this was the most surprising mission he'd ever encountered. Before he had much chance to think it over, Reed was giving him instructions on how to negotiate with a German general.

"Be careful," Reed cautioned. "If you give any sign that you understand German, the results may be fatal." Reed knew that the Germans might speak freely in front of Stewart, giving out secret information without knowing he understood the language. If the Germans realized that he had learned something confidential, they would take him prisoner—or perhaps even attack him on the spot.

Stewart nodded. He understood the risk.

When Sperl handed him notes describing the mission, Stewart scanned the text and immediately objected. "The note says 'emissary,'" he said. "Doesn't that make me sound too much like a spy?"

Sperl and the others burst out laughing. "Well . . . ?" Sperl said. "Sneaking across enemy lines on horseback to negotiate with the enemy? What else would you call it?"

They had a point. All joking aside, Stewart knew that this was a dangerous mission. He also knew he wasn't the first person asked to take a risk out here. Every man stepped up when his time came.

Ferdinand Sperl then typed up another fake document in the highest-sounding German he could muster. The letter designated Tom Stewart as a *plenipotentiary*: an officer of sufficient rank to accept the surrender of the station. To this document, someone added the flourish of General Patton's forged signature. He handed the documents to Captain Stewart.

When all was ready, Reed made a firm pronouncement. "Captain Stewart must be returned *safely* behind American lines within twenty-four hours."

Lessing nodded in agreement.

"If he fails to return by the deadline, American troops will advance on Hostau, guns blazing."

All three men understood what this meant. In a firefight for Hostau, the horses would be the losers.

Stewart scanned Lessing's guarded face, looking for a sign that he could trust the man. But the German was reserved and silent. No sign was forthcoming. Stewart would have to take this one on faith.

As Reed bade the men goodbye, he didn't say much, but Stewart could read his commander's expression. This mission mattered to him—he wanted to save the horses. The U.S. government would never officially approve of this mission—and if the mission went awry, Patton would take no public responsibility for the decision. Reed understood that saving these irreplaceable beasts was a choice *he* had to make, and a choice that came with exposing his soldiers to risk. In short, Hank Reed was trusting his gut.

By the time Stewart and Lessing arrived back at headquarters, the barracks was abuzz with the news: Captain Stewart was going to meet with a German general! Ready to leave in an officer's disguise and combat boots, he carefully pocketed the plenipotentiary document Sperl had given him.

It was already getting dark when Stewart set off with Rudolf Lessing, armed only with his basic knowledge of German, his impromptu documents, his pluck, and Lessing's sworn oath that Captain Stewart would be returned unharmed to regimental headquarters no later than noon the next day.

The two men rode the forester's motorcycle out of the 2nd Cavalry headquarters and headed to the forester's home deep in the woods. Soon they heard an airplane rumbling overhead. Lessing cut the motor and turned off the light.

"Don't worry, that's one of ours, Bed Check Charlie," Stewart reassured him.

"That won't stop him from shooting," Lessing said.

Stewart chuckled. From way up in the sky, that was probably true.

When they arrived at the forester's stable, Tom Stewart got his first look at the Lipizzaner stallion he would be riding. The horse had a well-formed head with a concave profile and a proud gleam in his soft, dark eyes. Stewart approached quietly, placing his hand gently on the animal's shoulder while murmuring a greeting. The stallion turned his head and gazed quizzically at the stranger. Lessing explained that this horse had been born at the royal Yugoslavian stud farm and once was the favorite mount of King Peter II.

The groom who had accompanied Lessing had long since headed back to Hostau on foot. Lessing watched as Stewart gathered the reins in one hand, put his left hand on the horse's powerful crest, and prepared to swing up into the saddle, each step in the correct manner of a practiced horseman. The horse always tested new riders, and the German wondered if this cowboy was up to the task. To Lessing's relief, Stewart vaulted neatly onto the horse's back. Once settled in the saddle, he gave the stallion a pat on the neck and grinned at Lessing.

It was already dark, and the pair had more than fifteen kilometers to cover. Rudofsky would be wondering where Lessing was, and already the clock was ticking on Stewart's deadline to return to the Americans.

The trail was narrow and threaded through the Bohemian Forest mountains. A ribbon of moonlight snaking through the trees helped illuminate their path, but there was always the possibility of wild lynx lurking in the dark shadows. Or, more frighteningly, men with guns might be peering at them from hideouts among the trees. But for now, they heard nothing but the rustling of pine needles and the horses' hoofbeats.

Stewart appeared relaxed in the saddle and held the reins in one hand, Western-style. Lessing still watched him warily, wondering if the American was adept enough to handle this nighttime ride on such a high-strung animal.

Eventually, they reached a barricade. On one side was a steep hill of rock; on the other side, a drop-off, so they couldn't go around it. Stewart walked his horse right up to it, looked it over, and then circled back around. Stewart whizzed past Lessing at a brisk canter, heading straight for the barrier, up and forward in his stirrups in a well-trained jumping position.

"That horse doesn't jump," Lessing called out. But Stewart was already airborne, maintaining his erect and balanced forward seat. Rudolf shrugged. He dismounted and led Indigo around the barrier on a narrow path around that Stewart hadn't noticed.

"So that's how you were supposed to do it," Stewart chuckled.

By the time they reached Hostau, it was two o'clock in the morning. Tom Stewart was miles behind enemy lines in Czechoslovakia. The small town's streets were eerily silent. Lessing took Stewart to his apartment, but when he arrived, he found the farm's other veterinarian, Wolfgang Kroll, on vigil outside his door, a machine gun slung across his lap.

17.

CHANGE OF HEART

During Lessing's brief absence, much had changed. A Nazi militia leader named General Schulze had come into town, accompanied by a ragtag band of young soldiers. The troop was using Hostau as its base—and they had issued an edict: *Bringing an American to the farm would now be regarded as an act of treason.*

Lessing listened to Kroll's news. His fellow veterinarian was known for telling tall tales. But this time, Lessing could see that he was deadly serious. In a few short hours, the situation had deteriorated from fragile to downright precarious. He quickly hid Stewart in his apartment and ran to find Rudofsky. Although it was the middle of the night, the stud farm director was waiting for him in the big house. Rudofsky confirmed Kroll's report: Indeed, General Schulze was now the highest-ranking officer at Hostau and was dead set against surrender to Americans.

"My hands are tied," Rudofsky said. "If I try to negotiate

with the Americans, or let on that one of them is here, then all three of us risk being shot for treason."

Lessing looked at him in disbelief. Twenty-four hours before, they had had a set plan—surrender was necessary to defend the horses. But if the Americans had to fight their way in, the horses' safety could not be guaranteed. If the men waited and did nothing, the Russians would arrive in a matter of days anyway. Exhausted and frustrated, Lessing returned to his apartment, filling Stewart in on the near-hopeless situation as the two shared a hot meal Lessing's wife prepared to warm their wind-chilled bones.

In the past twelve hours, Lessing had ridden more than thirty miles, had been held at gunpoint by the Americans, had escorted an American captain through woods studded with pockets of SS snipers, and now here he stood at a complete impasse. Weary but not daunted, he tried to keep his head.

As the two men talked urgently, neither could know exactly how close they were to the war's end. On Hitler's birthday just a week earlier, Joseph Goebbels, Reich minister of propaganda, had made a speech about Germany's impending defeat: "Germany is still the land of loyalty. . . . Never will history record that in these days a people deserted its führer or a führer deserted his people. And that is victory."

But Goebbels was dead wrong. The führer *would* indeed desert his people. Lessing and Stewart arrived at Hostau on April 28. In just two days, Hitler would commit suicide in his bunker, leaving his terrible empire gasping for its final breaths.

Lessing didn't sleep at all that night. At the rooster's first crow, he went to speak to the new officer at Hostau: General Schulze. But when he entered Schulze's presence, he did not have a chance to open his mouth before the red-faced commander started screaming at him. "How is it that you are negotiating with Americans?"

Lessing felt dread creep through him. The general had somehow gotten wind of his trip across the border.

"How dare you deceive the Germans?" Schulze continued. "I'm going to have you shot! You must be crazy!"

Lessing could see from the furious officer's face that he was not going to consider a compromise no matter how many lives were destroyed in the process. American trucks could be heard from Hostau, and Russians were just a day or two away. The Germans would be overcome any moment. The idea of fighting on when defeat was inevitable seemed to be illogically self-destructive, but General Schulze's attitude was not unusual in the German ranks.

However, to Lessing, the idea of fighting on when both Americans *and* Russians were approaching and defeat was inescapable simply made no sense. Lessing felt his horror at the general's suicidal stance turn first into anger, then into resolve. The veterinarian was only twenty-eight, and he had a lot more experience dealing with supposedly dumb beasts than with certifiably crazy, angry generals, but Lessing decided that even in the face of a death threat, it was time to speak his mind. The clock was ticking up at American headquarters, and if Stewart didn't reappear on schedule, American guns would be pointing straight at the stables.

"Sir . . . at Hostau, we are, first and foremost, here to maintain the horses. And it is thus our first duty to do everything in our powers to save them. We don't care about who wins the war on April twenty-seventh or twenty-eighth, because we should have won years ago. Now it is too late."

Lessing waited, expecting the general to explode again. To his surprise, Schulze responded in a calmer voice. "I can't make a decision on this matter with the Americans. You will have to go find my superior officer, the brigade commander, to ask for permission." With that, the general dismissed Lessing with a wave of his hand.

Lessing glanced anxiously at the clock and explained to the general that there was no time. Colonel Reed had made it clear: If the American had not been returned unharmed by noon on April 27, they would take aggressive action against Hostau.

"I will not let the American leave again. He stays!" the general said. "He's my prisoner of war."

As the morning haze cleared, the rising sun crept across the small village. Though the scene was still tranquil, it was clear to Lessing that something had to be done—and fast.

18.

LESSING TAKES CHARGE

At first light, Stewart, Lessing, and Kroll set off on horseback. As they rode through the stud farm's broad front gates, the village of Hostau appeared deceptively serene. Evergreen forests rose up the crest of distant hills. The horses' hooves clattered against the rounded, uneven stones. Soon enough, they arrived at their destination: a company command post located in a small house. Two soldiers guarded the door as a large man emerged from inside. It was the local *Gauleiter*, the ruling Nazi Party official, and on his face was an evil grin. Squaring his shoulders and raising his chin, Stewart approached and vaulted gracefully off the grand Lipizzaner stallion. Without even glancing at the Nazi boss, he tossed the reins at him as if this *Gauleiter* were a mere groom.

Lessing explained that they were seeking the brigade commander and needed permission to go to his headquarters. Stewart looked on, feet spread wide and arms folded. The *Gauleiter* hesitated, then finally told Lessing that the brigade commander was *Generalmajor* Weissenberger, and that his headquarters were located in the town of Klattau, about twenty-five miles to the southeast.

Glancing at their watches, Stewart and Lessing realized they had a problem. They had no chance of going all the way to Klattau and back and making Stewart's noon deadline. To solve this problem, Kroll offered to leave immediately on Indigo to let the Americans know that Stewart would be delayed. After transmitting the message, he would ride the horse back to the forester's house to wait for Lessing's return.

Lessing and Stewart thanked him and said goodbye before galloping back to the stud farm, where they swapped the horses for Lessing's motorcycle. With Stewart hastily disguised in a German raincoat and field cap, the pair zoomed off to *General-major* Weisenberger's headquarters in Klattau.

The greeting they received at the headquarters was chilly as they were briskly ushered inside. Seated at a bare table was a small man in a Wehrmacht uniform, flanked by German officers. Scanning the room, Lessing knew that any one of these officers might be a fanatical Nazi who could denounce him as a collaborator or even seize Stewart as a prisoner of war.

Though his heart was pounding, Tom Stewart remained steady. He looked straight into the eyes of the *Generalmajor*. The moment to make his case had arrived.

"The Americans wish to assist you in evacuating the horses safely back across the border to Bavaria," he announced, as Lessing translated. He offered greetings from General Patton and Colonel Reed before fishing in his pocket for the letter of introduction Sperl had typed. He smoothed it out on the table with a confident flourish.

A long pause followed as Weissenberger scrutinized the note. Speaking in rapid-fire German, the group appeared angry and couldn't seem to come to an agreement.

Lessing listened with increasing dismay. Speaking up for the first time, he explained that General Schulze had approved a plan and that the American captain had to be returned behind their lines no later than noon. All they needed was permission.

"The Americans' goal is to safeguard the horses and to preserve human life," Stewart added urgently.

Rather than reply, Weissenberger turned to Lessing in fury. "You never should have acted independently to cross enemy lines. The war is not even over! What you did is very risky!"

Lessing's face revealed nothing, but his blood was boiling. These men could not face the truth. Lessing thought of his wife, who had hidden the American officer in their home the night before, despite the risks. He thought of his daughter, Karen, who had been born into a topsy-turvy world through no fault of her own. He saw the American soldier sitting in front of him who had traveled across the world to help end a horrible mess of a war. Then Lessing turned his mind to the horses. He could imagine each of them: the eagle eyes of the Arabian Witez; the soft gaze of the white broodmare Madera; and the gentleness of his own Thoroughbred, Indigo, once a glamorous racehorse, who now served so faithfully.

When Lessing spoke, his words were disdainful and direct. "Oh, really? The war is not over? 'Berlin stays German. Vienna will be German again.' This is what we hear on the radio, but do you really believe this?"

The words tumbled out of him. If his superiors didn't like

what they were hearing, they could have him arrested or even killed. Lessing knew this, but he kept talking. "I fell for beautiful phrases like that for fourteen years. I have had enough. What we are doing here is madness. Should we push this mania even further so that we can destroy even those things in the end which were able to stay in one piece through all of this?"

A taut silence hung in the air until Weissenberger made an apathetic gesture and fell back into his chair. "Okay, fine. Do whatever you want."

Lessing insisted that Weissenberger write a letter stating his agreement. The *Generalmajor* agreed, and had two colonels write the note for him. His message said:

> *Herr General Schulze,*
>
> *I have taken it as my duty to allow the veterinary officer and the American captain to cross over enemy lines. However, the negotiation of Hostau stud farm cannot be determined by me and will thus require these men to return to Hostau.*
>
> *April 27, 13:40*

Finally, they had received the permission they needed. Once they arrived back at Hostau, Lessing showed Rudofsky the note, and then, with no time to make the cross-country ride to the Americans on horseback, Lessing and Stewart climbed on the motorcycle and sped back toward the forester's lodge. From there, the two parted company. Stewart continued back across American lines alone.

Up the forest path, Stewart spotted the welcome sight of an American jeep waiting for him. Back at headquarters, he found Wolfgang Kroll playing cards with the American soldiers and entertaining them with tales of his crazy exploits. Reed was quite relieved to see the young captain return in one piece.

When Stewart had not appeared by the promised noon deadline, Colonel Reed had started to set up a task force to rescue him. Then Kroll had arrived, and they had held him while awaiting Stewart's safe return. With the captain now safely in their midst, Reed had radioed General Patton for permission to send the task force to capture the stud farm at Hostau. He had received Patton's terse reply: "Get them. Make it fast."

On April 28, 1945, General Patton confided to his diary, "Personally, I cannot see that there is very much more glory in this war." Clearly, Patton did not yet see the glory of what was about to unfold.

Lessing waited for Kroll for several hours at the forester's house. At last he mounted Indigo and headed toward home. As the trail neared a large manor house, he caught sight of the gentleman who lived there. He had cared for this man's horses before. The man waved him down and, perhaps noticing that Lessing looked exhausted, offered him a bite to eat.

Lessing hadn't slept in over thirty hours. Until he heard the kindly offer, he had not even been aware of his own fatigue. He decided to stop for a moment, and he was grateful for the bowl of hot soup that was placed before him. But before Lessing had a chance to finish the meal, the phone rang. The man quickly passed along the news: American forces were rolling toward the village—and they were already just a few miles outside Hostau.

Forgetting his fatigue and hunger, Lessing jumped back onto Indigo. If he did not arrive in time with the message that the Americans were on their way, General Schulze might start firing on them. Then the Americans would enter Hostau with guns ablaze. Lessing urged Indigo into a gallop and headed back down toward the village as fast as the horse would carry him.

19.

THE TANKS ARE COMING

The morning after his safe return to his American army head-quarters, Captain Tom Stewart was mounted up again—this time in a jeep, leading a task force of about seventy men from the 42nd Squadron of the 2nd Cavalry. During their negotiations, the Germans had promised Stewart that their troops would not defend the stud farm but had not guaranteed them safe passage. The Americans would have to fight off any resistance encountered on the way there. Armed with two tanks and two assault guns, the group was headed over the border into Czechoslovakia. Only the officers knew where they were going and why.

As the small task force headed out, they were aware of the dangers of operating behind enemy lines. Small bands of roving Germans were scattered throughout the area. Some were fight-to-the-death SS snipers. Many others were defectors looking to steal gas and provisions so they could flee to Germany in advance of the Russians. One thing was certain: Anyone Stewart's men came across out here would not be friendly.

Shortly after crossing the border into Czechoslovakia, Stewart's troop faced a brief flurry of gunfire. Returning fire with their machine guns, they quickly subdued the inferior force. Stewart had a funny feeling that the same officers who had given their word to him the day before in Klattau were now shooting at him; he was not surprised when he found Colonel Trost, one of the men who had signed Weissenberger's letter of safe passage just a day before, among the wounded. The opposition quelled, Stewart and his men continued slowly on their way.

Meanwhile, Hubert Rudofsky could hear the American tanks approaching Hostau. People on the farm milled around anxiously. Rudofsky scanned the horizon, hoping that Lessing would return soon.

It was then that he saw General Schulze, clearly agitated, hurrying toward his large Mercedes. To Rudofsky's surprise, a moment later, the Mercedes careened out the farm's front gates. Schulze and his men had fled, knowing that they could not last against the arriving Americans. Just then, Rudofsky saw Lessing and Indigo tearing over the crest of the hill. Arriving at the stud farm a moment later, the veterinarian recounted breathlessly that American tanks were just a few miles away. By then, the Nazi general was already gone, leaving nothing but a plume of dust behind him.

Rudofsky's thoughts strayed to his family eight miles away

in an area still under Nazi control. The Hitler Youth and local militia were preparing to mount a final defense. Just the week before, Rudofsky had seen his nephew camped behind a bunker with a gun in hand. Ulli, a slight, light-blond boy with a bright face, was by now a few days shy of ten. Rudofsky had taken the gun from his nephew's hands and told him, "This is no business for you." He hoped that the boy had the sense to keep himself out of trouble.

Honor-bound to remain with the horses, Rudofsky pushed his personal concerns out of his mind as he waited for the Americans to arrive. He knew nothing of the approaching enemy except what he'd heard over secret radio broadcasts. These unknown men would soon hold the horses' destiny in their hands—and Rudofsky had no way of knowing what they would choose to do with them. The weight of his responsibility hung heavily upon him. Hubert Rudofsky would go down in history as the man who gave away the emperor's horses. He had chosen to put their safety first. Only time would tell if he had made the right decision.

Hastily, Rudofsky pulled down the portrait of Hitler and hid anything with a Nazi symbol. Together, he and Lessing hung white bedsheets out the windows to signal surrender. Grasping another sheet between them, they strode out the farm's front gates and headed to meet their conquerors.

A second troop of American soldiers took another path to Hostau. They were prepared to provide Tom Stewart and his crew with reinforcements. In command of one platoon was one of Reed's most reliable men, Captain William Donald "Quin" Quinlivan, a career soldier in the old horse cavalry. Quinlivan had a soft core and a tough demeanor—he adored all animals, but he knew how to ride herd on his men. Before they had set off, Quinlivan had overheard some grumbling about their mission; everyone knew the war was almost over and nobody wanted to get himself killed now, with an end finally in sight.

Quinlivan also had his own concerns, but he kept them to himself. As they rattled along under the low morning sky, he was thinking about his family back home, especially his mother. He hated to think how she would feel if she found out she'd lost him over some foolish mission to rescue a bunch of horses.

As their vehicles rumbled through the forest, Lieutenant Quinlivan stayed on high alert, snapping to attention at the slightest movement or sound. The forest around them remained dark and still, until, finally, they emerged from the woods into bright sunlight. After traveling a few miles, the village of Hostau spread out before them. Not a soul was on the streets. There, in the distance, was the horse farm with its rows of stables and neatly fenced pastures. Groups of white horses were scattered across the fields, some with coal-black foals at their side. At the sound of the approaching troops, they spun and tore off at a gallop, seeming to float on the wind. Quinlivan sucked in his breath with appreciation. Cautiously, he and his men proceeded down the hill. Soon they came upon two Germans in full dress uniform: a tall man with round spectacles and a proud, guarded face—Hubert Rudofsky— and a slim veterinary officer—Rudolf Lessing. Between them, they held a white bedsheet for surrender. A moment later, the

Americans drove through the gates that led into the horse farm.

Hubert Rudofsky gave the order: The German flag came down. The Stars and Stripes shimmied up the flagpole and began to flutter in the wind.

Hitler's secret super-stud farm was under American rule.

20.

THE FALLEN

Just a day after Tom Stewart spent the night huddled in Lessing's apartment, he found himself in a new position: commanding officer of the village of Hostau. Horses gazed serenely at the American soldiers in green fatigues and combat boots as the men established checkpoints and inspected for enemy elements. Most of the grooms at Hostau were German prisoners of war—Russians, Poles, and Yugoslavs as well as a smattering of other Allies. With the coming of the Americans, they would soon be released and sent back to their ranks.

Late that afternoon, Hank Reed rode up the driveway of the Hostau stud farm in his battered green jeep. After 281 days of battle, Hank Reed had arrived back where he'd started—among horses. Stewart and Quinlivan greeted him and introduced him to the farm's German military staff, who were now being held as American prisoners of war.

Colonel Rudofsky stood at the head of the line. He studied

the American commander's face, wondering what kind of person he was about to encounter.

Reed walked down the line of conquered officers, trying to set them at ease. Rudofsky was surprised that the man's manner was friendly yet respectful. The first order of business was to tour the farmland. O'Leary drove them around the stud farm, as far as the outlying pastures. In the fields, white mares grazed peacefully, while their dark-coated foals cavorted at their sides.

The next order of business was a tour of the stables. Sperl translated for the Americans as Rudofsky gave detailed information about the farm's operations. Reed encouraged the enlisted men to come along and have a look. The colonel's enthusiasm for the horses was unmistakable, and it soon rubbed off on the rest of the group.

When the tour of the grounds and pastures was finished, it was time for the presentation of Hostau's finest jewels: the stallions. When Witez was led from the stable, his shiny coat created a halo of light around him. His tapered ears flicked back and forth; his dark eyes seemed to contain infinite depths; and his hooves seemed almost to float above the ground. Witez's bright expression spoke to something deep inside Reed.

Satisfied that the stud farm was secured, Reed left Stewart with a small task force made up of several platoons of soldiers. He instructed Rudofsky, Lessing, and Kroll to continue operations as usual, now under Stewart's command.

A few days later, Tom Stewart got word from his forward patrols that a group of Germans who had fired on them on the way to the stud farm had reassembled into an organized force. The group was advancing on the farm itself. Stewart and Quinlivan assembled their small group in an attempt to push the advancing Germans as far away from the horses as possible. To strengthen his numbers, Stewart drafted some of the released prisoners of war, including a Palestinian man and a Maori man from New Zealand still wearing their POW garb, to join with the Americans.

The battle raged for five hours, until the Germans retreated into the woods and moments later came pouring out between the trees, carrying white flags. Tired, shaken, and deeply relieved, Stewart and Quinlivan had defeated the last bits of German resistance.

On the morning of Monday, April 30, while Tom Stewart was fighting off the German attackers, Hank Reed was in Schwarzenfeld, about eighty kilometers southwest of Hostau. Colonel Reed and three other officers of the XII Corps, to which the 2nd Cavalry belonged, were being honored with the French Legion of Honor and the Croix de Guerre. The day before, General Patton had visited XII Corps headquarters and told their commander that the war might be over in the next day or two. Reed stood at attention, eyes forward, as the heavy French sword tapped his shoulder. He was eager to get this over with, impatient to return to his men and their captured prize.

By late afternoon of that day, Reed was back at Hostau, pleased with the work that Stewart had done in his absence. Just like everyone else in the Third Army, Reed had learned many bleak things about the human race over the past twelve months. He had heard about the atrocities that the army had uncovered when they liberated the first concentration camps—the horrors of train cars filled with corpses, and the scores of prisoners, as weak and thin as scarecrows. But somehow he had been spared seeing those particular evils firsthand and instead had been given the task of freeing these beautiful horses. It was an unlikely and astonishing stroke of grace.

The war had destroyed many things, but one of the worst casualties was the loss of hope for a peaceful world. That day, Hank Reed knew that for all of the sadness and loss and pain he had seen, he would accomplish at least one positive thing: Lovely and unbloodied, these horses were going to gallop safely into the postwar world.

21.

THE AMERICANS

While Hank Reed's convoys headed toward Hostau to rescue the horses, two hundred kilometers away, in Austria, Alois Podhajsky listened to the distant sounds of gunfire, certain that the village of St. Martin would be captured within hours. Would all of his hard work to save the stallions be lost as these final moments played out? Since communication with Hostau had broken down over the last few weeks, he had been concerned about the broodmares, but at the moment, he was most worried about his white stallions.

Shortly after General Weingart's visit, Podhajsky had been appointed commandant of the defense sector St. Martin. His job was to defend the Austrian village for Germany. Podhajsky vowed to himself that he would indeed defend St. Martin—by doing everything he could to aid a rapid and peaceful surrender. Minimizing violence and bloodshed was his priority.

Night was falling. The sounds of fighting, still distant and intermittent, had ceased for the time being. Podhajsky was crossing the castle grounds when the mayor of the town appeared, asking for orders to gather the Volkssturm—the national militia—to fight the Americans. This was precisely what Podhajsky was determined to avoid at all costs. The way he saw it, if anyone tried to defend the village, the Americans would come in shooting. Then both the civilians *and* the horses would be endangered.

But as the designated head of the defense sector, Podhajsky could not let on that he had no intention of fighting back. If he showed his cards, he might soon be attacked, unable to do anything further to protect his precious stallions. So Podhajsky had to make the local Nazis think he was playing along.

Thinking quickly, he devised a scheme to divert the mayor's attention. The mayor would want to protect his own business—a butcher shop—so the colonel told him to divide up the Volkssturm troops and station them in front of the town's shops to prevent looting. The mayor, in eager agreement, hurried away to put Podhajsky's plan into motion.

Next, two Nazi Party officials appeared. They had orders, they said, from the *Kreisleiter*, the regional Nazi authority, to block all of the roads around the town. They wanted Podhajsky to order the troops to put up barricades. Podhajsky cringed. The Americans were known to double their firepower if they came across any barricades. If Americans unleashed their powerful tanks directly upon the barriers, the village would be severely damaged or destroyed. Buying time, he told them to post guards at checkpoints but to leave the roads open.

Soon the *Kreisleiter* arrived back at the castle, and Podhajsky was summoned to the local Nazi Party officials' office.

When Podhajsky entered their office, the Nazi leaders, pale and anxious, greeted him in stony silence. The door banged open, and the *Kreisleiter* and two armed SS men burst into the room, breaking the silence with a cry of "Heil Hitler."

"Have the barriers been put up yet?" the *Kreisleiter* shouted.

Like a fish gasping for air, the senior official opened his mouth, but no words came out.

Podhajsky spoke instead, careful to keep his voice even. "No, the barriers have not been put up yet. Otherwise your car would not have been able to get in here."

"Why were my orders not carried out?" The *Kreisleiter's* face was flushed with anger.

The room bristled with tension. The *Kreisleiter*, flanked by his two heavily armed henchmen, stared at Podhajsky. The colonel calmly met his gaze. Everyone else in the room shrank back, wondering what was going to happen next.

Podhajsky felt the cool stock of his pistol and decided he would not go down without a fight. His mind spun through the possibilities. He knew he was one hair trigger away from being shot and made an example of. If that happened, who would protect his horses? He steadied himself, imagining the faces of his beloved Pluto and Africa.

Podhajsky swallowed. In the calmest voice he could summon, he lied, and pretended as though the Germans had already stopped the Americans, hoping that the *Kreisleiter* would believe him. "After our troops brought the advance of the Americans to a halt, I didn't think that any useful purpose would be served by closing the streets, since this might hinder the freedom of movement of our own soldiers ... But I have had the barriers manned by the Volkssturm, and made the necessary arrangements for them to be closed in the shortest possible time when I give the order."

The *Kreisleiter* said nothing but appeared to be thinking. Podhajsky waited, hoping his bluff would work.

The SS officers held their guns, ready to spring into action if their leader appeared dissatisfied. But the *Kreisleiter* seemed to accept Podhajsky's explanation. "Then everything is in good order," he said.

He spun on his heel and strode out the door and into the night. With Nazi flags fluttering, his shiny black car drove off to the next village. Apparently he was satisfied that Colonel Podhajsky would defend this one against Americans to the death.

Alois Podhajsky had donned the uniform of the German Wehrmacht in 1938. Back then, he had been one of the top equestrian competitors in the world. When he took leadership of the Spanish Riding School of Vienna, he had pledged to safeguard his homeland's premier equestrian institution. Nearly seven years had passed, years of constant compromise—and yet the success of his mission was not assured. In the next few hours or days, his ultimate measure as a soldier and as a man would be decided. Would he succeed in saving the horses for Austria? How would history regard his many compromises? Through all of this, it was his stallions, Pluto and Africa and all of the others, that had served as his guidepost. Podhajsky took off his German uniform and pulled on civilian clothing. Hastily bundling up the uniform, he hid it. An unnatural silence hung over the village. There was nothing to do but wait.

All night, they could hear German troops and soldiers leaving town. By morning, the village was quiet. Around lunchtime, one of Podhajsky's riders came racing in: *The Americans were almost there.*

At his signal, Podhajsky's riders shed their uniforms and donned civilian clothes. Verena took the cast-off uniforms and hid them in one of the castle's large drawing rooms. Podhajsky instructed his riders to hand over their weapons, then quickly retreat to the stables and stay out of sight.

During the next few hours, a frenzy swirled outside St. Martin. American soldiers rounded up any Germans in uniform. Freed prisoners of war started to riot and loot. Podhajsky and his riders were prepared to take action if necessary, but the ruckus stayed outside the closed stable doors. In their stalls, Africa, Pluto, and the other stallions raised their heads at the noise. By the end of the day, the American troops had restored order. All was calm again. At long last, the bitter days of Nazi domination had ended.

But safety still was not assured for the beleaguered horses. The Americans had taken over an area that was on the brink of chaos, teeming with refugees and POWs, displaced people who needed aid, and Nazis trying to escape detection.

The next day, the roads into the village of St. Martin were clogged with American vehicles and important-looking soldiers bustling around. Word was circulating through the village—the American brigadier general William A. Collier of the XX Corps would be arriving soon to set up headquarters in the castle. Among the multitude of problems, how was Podhajsky going to convince these Americans that the horses were important?

22.

THE GENERALS

Podhajsky was filled with a deep sense of dread. The animals were no longer in immediate physical danger, but they had been cast adrift.

The decision to leave Vienna had been gut-wrenching, the moments when Podhajsky had put his stallions at risk some of the most terrifying of his life. The horses and riders had survived the war, but their institution had never been more at risk. He had had no news of the fate of the mares at Hostau— isolated in St. Martin, he was not yet aware of the American colonel's capture of the stud farm. Nor did he know whether the elegant Viennese riding hall had survived. But his most im- mediate concern was whom to ask to procure more food and grain for the horses.

For months before the evacuation, Podhajsky had been careful to stockpile food, reducing the horses' rations slightly and requesting extra grain. That surplus was nearly gone, and who could guarantee that the Americans would think it impor-

tant to support the Spanish Riding School? This old institution might be seen as nothing more than a relic of a defeated
order, as outdated as the Austro-Hungarian Empire itself.

Podhajsky passed through the stables, greeting each of the
horses by name and handing out lumps of sugar. He lingered at
the stalls of Pluto, the young stallion with so much potential,
and Africa, with his unusually sensitive temperament. They
were alive and healthy, but would they ever perform again?
Would the world ever have another opportunity to see the brilliance these two animals had to offer?

Outside the quiet stables, Americans were rushing around
in a fever pitch of preparations. Suddenly, one of Podhajsky's
riders came barreling up to him. "There is an American officer
inquiring after you," the rider said, out of breath. "He wants to
see you immediately. He saw you ride in the Olympics and he
wants to meet you and see how you are doing!"

Podhajsky felt his heart leap just a little. Perhaps he would
finally find a sympathetic ear for his cause.

Hurrying down to the stables, he found the American major
who had asked for him by name and remembered his incredible
ride at the Berlin Olympics. With him were Brigadier General
Collier and the corps commander, General Walton Walker.

Walker spoke up with an idea. His boss, General George
Patton, was coming up for a look around the next day, and
Walker thought he'd like to see Podhajsky's stallions. Every-
one knew that Patton had a strong interest in horses. Could
Podhajsky possibly put on a show for the general? Tomorrow?

When Podhajsky heard the well-known name of General
Patton, famed leader of the Third Army as well as a fellow
former Olympian, he felt a brief moment of elation that was

replaced swiftly by crushing doubt. Under normal circumstances, the riders prepared for their shows for months. How
could they possibly be ready for a show so soon? Then again,
how could he refuse? Hesitatingly, he agreed.

That night, the first of the American occupation, Podhajsky
barely slept. His bed was a child's cot that did not fit his long
legs, but even worse, his mind was spinning with worries about
the show he had promised to put on. Getting the attention of
an American in the high command was his very best shot at
securing help for the school, but how could he put together a
worthy demonstration on such short notice? They were missing
a number of riders—the ones whom the army had pressed into
military service. But even with the participation of those available, the show would demand so much of the horses. Like all
highly trained athletes, the stallions could not be kept at peak
training except during brief periods of time. Recently their life
had been topsy-turvy and their training had been haphazard at
best. The casual observer might not know the difference, but an
experienced horseman could. And Patton would be watching
the performance with the keen eye of an expert.

The next few days were a flurry of activity. Podhajsky asked
volunteers to help clean the courtyard and indoor riding hall.
They unpacked the loudspeakers used for piped-in music and,
with the help of the soldiers, strung up electric lights that shone
cheerfully inside the dreary riding hall.

Podhajsky could contemplate everything that had happened to him in the last few weeks. His struggle for permission
to leave Vienna. The air raids on the trains. Convincing Nazis
not to fight back when the Americans arrived. That moment
when he stepped out of the hated Wehrmacht uniform. His

intense relief that the war was finally over. *Plus* the knowledge that he and his horses were exiled from their home and might not ever be able to return. But to think of all these things would have completely overwhelmed his emotions. Instead, Podhajsky plunged into preparation for the show.

He put Pluto and Africa through their paces, testing to see what each was willing to give. Pluto was flighty, as usual, but capable of brilliance. Africa tried to please his master. Despite all the disruption and lack of proper training, Podhajsky found that his horses seemed to sense the urgency and responded by offering their best. He watched each of his riders and the horses in turn and was able to map out a program for the performance— one that took into consideration the small space, the reduced number of riders, and the degree of difficulty of the movements being asked of their mounts. He simply could not demand too much when the horses weren't ready.

Finally, the American military entourage arrived with a sweep of pomp and circumstance. It was impossible not to notice General Patton, who strode in with the confident air of a conquering commander, raising his hand as he passed the row of riders lined up to greet him. He and his group found their places on the platform that had been reserved for them.

It was time for the performance to begin. A million thoughts whirled through Podhajsky's mind. Not just: *Will the horses be good enough?* but also, deeper down: *Even if they're good enough, will anyone care?* Would these strangers, these foreigners, be able to fully recognize the animals' extraordinary gifts?

The art of classical riding was one of subtlety. While audiences were always impressed to see the leaps and jumps that were the airs above the ground, true horsemen knew that the

real achievement of the Spanish Riding School was its celebration of harmony, peace, and symmetry: the seemingly effortless
display that could be achieved only after years of training and
dedication on the part of horses and riders alike. Podhajsky put
his faith in the fact that Patton was a horseman, but even more
than that, he put his faith in his horses and in the spell they
seemed to cast. Suddenly, Podhajsky thought of something
General Erich Weingart had said to him at their last meeting:
The horses will work their magic....

The music started.

General George Smith Patton sat on the viewing platform,
watching this special performance that had been put together
to entertain him. He and Podhajsky had something very important in common: Patton had competed in the modern pentath-
lon in the 1912 Olympic Games in Stockholm, and Podhajsky
had competed in dressage in 1936. So much had changed for
both of the men since then, but the love for horses had not diminished in either of them.

Two riders opened the show with a pas de deux, a choreographed pair performance. From his position, Podhajsky could
see that the sequence was proceeding flawlessly, but his gaze
kept flitting back to General Patton in an effort to analyze his
expression. The general appeared blasé, almost bored, as he
watched. Podhajsky might not have known that this style of
equestrianism was different from the kind of riding that Patton was used to. The American school favored the so-called
forward method, where the horses moved in a more "natural"
way, with head and neck extended. The training of the collected

horse—which kept its hindquarters well beneath, its crest high, and the nose almost perpendicular to the ground, its gaits well controlled beneath the rider—was distinctly European. For a foxhunter and polo player like George Patton, this style of riding was quite foreign.

Next was the quadrille, in which the horses performed in formation, as tightly choreographed as a drum corps. Surely this would make an impression. Mounted on Africa, Podhajsky led off this display of ultimate horsemanship: eight horses and eight riders performing in absolute harmony.

When the quadrille ended, Podhajsky patted Africa, rubbed his neck, and whispered a kind word in his ear. The horse had performed perfectly, even in these inelegant conditions.

Verena came back to the staging area and whispered to her husband: She was sure that Patton and the others were enjoying the program. The general no longer looked bored—he was leaning forward attentively, and the other spectators appeared enthralled.

If Patton and Podhajsky had known each other personally, the two Olympians most likely would have recognized in each other an intensity and determination. Just as Podhajsky knew how to put on an equestrian show, Patton himself was once in charge of the army's biggest equestrian spectacle—the Society Circus, held every year at Fort Meyer, Virginia. Patton's demonstration had showcased some of the army's most advanced trick riding, including highly skilled acrobatics performed on horseback. But all of that was long in the past for Patton, who was now famous for turning the army away from horses in favor of the technological advances—including jeeps, tanks, and other motorized vehicles—that had helped the Allies win the war.

Still, Patton, of all people, had an idea of how much work it took to put on a show such as this one.

To perform the finale, Podhajsky had again chosen Africa. He hoped he had made the right decision: This was the first time his excitable stallion had ever performed alone. Silently, with just a light touch of the reins, the pressure of his legs, and his weight in the saddle, Podhajsky communicated with his stallion, his partner in crime, his companion: This was the most important moment of both of their lives.

Most people in the audience would never know anything about these horses or the hardships they had suffered, but they would see that this performance was about beauty and harmony, peace and mutual understanding. Each of these qualities seemed to have been lost in the struggle, chaos, and overwhelming sadness of the war. Podhajsky believed that these horses could help people, just for a moment, tap into something beautiful that spoke to all of humankind.

Always brilliant in his movements, Africa sparkled with animation today. The Americans on the sidelines were riveted and could not take their eyes off the pair. Podhajsky stole a glance at the general's face and saw that Patton was indeed falling under the horse's spell. Podhajsky and Africa passed seamlessly through intricate maneuvers—pirouettes, flying lead changes, lateral movements—not looking like man and beast, but appearing as one. Podhajsky realized that the enthusiasm of the assembled spectators was growing as each exercise that Africa performed was met with applause. Podhajsky felt the harnessed power of the stallion beneath him; Africa somehow seemed to sense that he was dancing for his life.

Podhajsky and Africa turned up the center line of the arena, directly toward Patton, who was seated in the middle of the viewing stand. First, they approached in the movement known as *passage*—a floating trot where the horse exaggerates the suspension of each stride. Then Podhajsky collected the stallion into a *piaffe*, an even more difficult movement, in which a horse lifts his feet and trots in place.

At last they came to a halt. Neapolitano Africa stopped completely square, his hooves lined up as if standing on an invisible line. Podhajsky removed his bicorne hat and looked directly at General George Patton, who stood and returned a salute.

As Podhajsky later wrote in his memoir, "It was one of the most important moments in my life. In a little Austrian village in a decisive hour two men faced each other, both having fought for the Olympic crown for their countries. . . . Although they now met on such unequal terms, the one as a triumphant conqueror in a war waged with such bitterness, the other as a member of a defeated nation."

"Honorable General," Podhajsky said in English. "I thank you for the honor you have done the Spanish Riding School. This ancient Austrian institution is now the oldest riding school in the world, and has managed to survive wars and revolutions throughout the centuries, and by good fortune, has lived also through the recent years of upheaval." None of those assembled knew just how true that was. Among the numerous heartbreaks of this terrible war, the innocent horses shot, abused, and killed would not rank among the worst atrocities—but somehow, the killing of innocent beasts, domesticated animals who existed only for man's beauty and pleasure, seemed to highlight the barbaric and depraved depths to which man had allowed himself to sink.

"The great American nation," Podhajsky continued, "which has been singled out to save European culture from destruction, will certainly interest itself also in this ancient academy . . . I'm sure I shall not plead in vain in asking you, General, for your special protection and help; for protection for the Spanish Riding School. . . ."

Patton at first seemed a bit surprised by Podhajsky's words. He paused and whispered something to the undersecretary of war. Turning back to Podhajsky, he said, "I hereby place the Spanish Riding School under the official protection of the American army in order to restore it to a newly risen Austria."

At midnight on May 8, 1945, the Germans would officially surrender and the war in Europe would be over.

But for Podhajsky and Africa, the war ended the moment they strode together from the ring, having triumphed over their own fear and uncertainty, to step together into a new age.

23.

THE CRAZIEST CARAVAN IN THE WORLD

Hostau, Czechoslovakia, May 15, 1945

Captain Tom Stewart looked around the stable courtyard in Hostau, Czechoslovakia, with wonder. Before him, Prince Ammazov, leader of the Cossacks, was mounted on one of his Russian Kabardins. His ten-year-old daughter, already an expert rider, was mounted beside him on a sturdy Panje pony. The remainder of his Cossack troop kept watch over the horses.

The German former staff of Hostau, now American POWs wearing civilian clothing, stood by with checklists, calling out instructions. Uniformed American GIs, most of whom had little experience with horses, worked together to ready hundreds of the world's most beautiful animals for departure. A herd of jeeps and tanks were loaded down with horse equipment—halters, bridles, and harnesses—and the men's possessions. Everyone was leaving.

Only Rudofsky, the former stud farm master, would stay behind with his family. Not until after the American 38th Infantry had taken his town had he heard the frightening story about how young Ulli had hidden with his classmates inside the walls of the local castle as the American tanks approached. With the guns pointed straight at them, the boy's teacher had handed him a strip of white cloth and pushed him outside in front of the others, whispering, "Americans don't shoot children." Fortunately, Ulli had survived the war unscathed, but Rudofsky wouldn't dare abandon the boy, whose father was still missing.

Besides, Rudofsky was convinced that with the Nazis defeated, Czechoslovakia had no more enemies, and its future looked bright. Before the war, Czechoslovakia had been a democracy, and Rudofsky believed it would become one again— a place with room for all.

Lessing tried to talk him out of staying. The two men carried on heated conversations out of earshot of the Americans.

"You are naive," Lessing said. "The Czech . . . hate Germans— with good reason—and you are an ethnic German."

Rudofsky was adamant. He had done his duty to ensure the safety of the horses. He would not abandon his family or the country of his birth. He would follow the horses only as far as the border.

Hank Reed had plenty of experience with large-scale horse operations. But moving so many horses without the proper equipment or trucks could be dangerous. The stress of the journey might send the pregnant mares into labor. The horses might not cooperate. What was more, the crew assembled to move the horses was a motley assortment of people, many of whom had been sworn enemies just a few weeks earlier. On top of the horses and men, Reed had agreed that for humanitarian reasons, families who wanted to hitch a ride with the caravan could come along, bringing their children and personal belongings.

Quinlivan outfitted makeshift trucks to move the horses. They were hardly the padded train cars or specially fitted-out horse trailers normally used to transport valuable equines, but they were the best the men could do. Only the mares closest to foaling and the newborns too young to walk would get to ride. The rest of the horses would be safer traveling on foot, herded in groups—cowboy-style—across the border.

Since entering Czechoslovakia, Reed and the 2nd Cavalry had been dancing a tricky two-step with the Russians. Reed had a confrontation with a Russian general who claimed that his orders were to keep moving west into territory already held by American troops. Reed had stood up and, sternly shaking his finger, told the Russian in no uncertain terms that he should not advance because American guns were still loaded. In that instance, the Russian had agreed to detour around the American-held town. But it wasn't the only time the Americans at Hostau came up against the Russians.

The situation on the ground in western Czechoslovakia remained confusing and chaotic as the two giant armies, Russian and American, crowded up against each other, sharing space with terrified local citizens, floods of newly captured prisoners of war, and roadways filled with lines of weary refugee families fleeing west. Mob violence broke out.

The horses needed to be moved quickly into American-held territory; otherwise, Reed would have no say about what became of them. A Czechoslovakian representative had already visited the farm, seeming eager to make a claim that the horses belonged to the Czech government—a claim that Rudofsky, the only man with knowledge of the horses located at Hostau before the war, roundly disputed. The Americans could provide protection on the roadways leading out of Hostau, but the dangerous part would be to get the horses safely across a border manned by Czechoslovakian guards.

Reed knew that if he messed this up and the horses didn't make it back to Germany in one piece, he would go down in history as the most inept cavalryman ever let loose in Europe. He would not just disappoint General Patton, he would create a public relations nightmare. He had carried his men all the way through the war and out the other side. Rescuing these horses was the last big job that he had been given—and he was determined to see it through.

When all was ready, Tom Stewart led the procession. Following closely behind were the trucks transporting three hundred precious mares and foals. A thunder of hoofbeats filled the air as this parade crowded Hostau's narrow main street. Witez was among them, his eyes bright, tail aloft. Placid white mares, frisky colts, bounding Arabians, and stocky Russian horses— they were all heading out of town. From the truck beds, tiny foals struggling to balance on spindly legs peered with wonder through the truck's slats.

Witez set off eagerly, eyes bright, tail aloft. On his back, one of the cavalry riders, a cowboy who hailed from Idaho, looked like he was having the time of his life. Few of the horses stabled at Hostau, horses used for breeding, were trained to be ridden under saddle, but Witez was one. The bay had been given the important job of riding herd on the young stallions, the group that would be most excitable.

It was hard to believe that just two weeks earlier, Stewart and his men had fought their way into Hostau. Now, in addition to the men of the 2nd Cavalry, hundreds of American soldiers lined the streets to allow them to pass safely. At each intersection, American vehicles guarded the roads.

Yet the group had barely gotten started when trouble began to brew. Before they'd left the village limits, the young stallions got too close to the mares, and the handlers lost control. Quinlivan steadied Lotnik as he watched a couple of stallions break loose from the group and gallop away. The horses hightailed it across the fields, back in the direction of the stables. There was no time to send someone after them—every hand was needed in the caravan; they would have to retrieve them later.

Tom Stewart stayed up front in his jeep, sticking close to the trucks. The road crossed flower-studded meadows, plunged them deep into forest and then back out along sunny trails. Lessing and Kroll circulated among the groups tending to the horses that needed attention. They were footsore and wounded, unaccustomed to walking so far.

The second day was bright and clear. A sense of optimism grew through the group. Rudolf Lessing, mounted on Indigo, rode toward the front of the first large herd. Before long, they could see a small burg in the distance, and Lessing's heart skipped a beat when he realized that soon they would cross the border between Czechoslovakia and Germany. An elegant arched bridge led over the Chamb river; once on the other side, they would be in Bavaria, now officially an American protectorate.

As the first group of horses and riders approached the checkpoint, Lessing saw an armed Czech border control officer manning the gate. As the caravan got closer, the border guards ordered the gate shut. They pointed their guns directly at the men and horses.

The horses began prancing and pawing, not understanding why they couldn't move forward. Lessing grew increasingly nervous. The Czech partisans manning the barricades were shouting that the horses could not go through. *You have no permission to remove horses or any other property from Czechoslovakian territory*, they told the American army men. Lessing knew very well that these horses were *not* Czech property—they had all been brought from other countries, and they were now under American control. But as a German prisoner of war, he was afraid to say anything for fear of making matters worse.

Quinlivan sized up the situation. He saw hot tempers, pointed guns, and snorting and pawing horses whose coiled energy was about to explode. Quinlivan swiftly took the matter in hand. He radioed the troop's tanks, which had just pulled up at the tail of the convoy, and told them to point their guns directly at the barricades.

"Open that gate, or I'll open it for you," Quinlivan said firmly. The guns and guards faced off. Finally the surly border guard jerked his head and the barrier lifted.

Galloping and trotting, dancing and prancing, showing the gaits for which they were so rightly famed, the horses streamed forward, the sunlight glinting on their backs, across the bridge and over the border into the American protectorate in Germany. Among the surging horses, Witez's burnished bay coat stood out. Throughout the ride, he had been the perfect mentor. He seemed to be telling the frisky young stallions to settle down and get a move on, that this was serious business.

At the border, Hubert Rudofsky stood straight and tall in his unfamiliar civilian clothes, holding a clipboard. With a businesslike demeanor, he checked off the name of each horse, every one of which he knew by sight, as they passed, until soon they were all too far off to see.

With a heavy heart, Rudofsky said farewell and returned to Hostau. Now the air seemed drained of sound, leaving only a hollow emptiness. The long aisles of the whitewashed stables stood empty and hushed. At forty-eight years old, Rudofsky had nowhere to go but back to his mother's house in the neighboring town of Bischofteinitz. At least his nephew, Ulli, who had held the white flag as he surrendered to the American forces, would be eager to welcome him home.

On the afternoon of May 16, Stewart, Quinlivan, and Lessing finally arrived at their destination of Kötzting, Germany, with more than three hundred exhausted, footsore purebreds. They could not have found a setting less hospitable for sensitive, pampered horses. The small town was bursting at the seams. The seventeen thousand German prisoners of war were encamped under guard in empty fields. Adding to the chaos was a flood of refugees—German speakers who had fled Bohemia and Silesia in advance of the Russians and now sought shelter anywhere they could find it.

All of the horses had made the journey safely, but as Lessing, Quinlivan, and Stewart surveyed the poor conditions in Kötzting, they knew they still faced a mighty challenge. Keeping the horses fed, watered, and safe from thieves would take the utmost alertness from a group already overwhelmed by other demands.

Hank Reed was not on hand to witness their arrival; his headquarters remained in Czechoslovakia. He had taken over the castle belonging to Baron von Skoda, owner of the Skoda Works, one of Germany's biggest providers of arms and explosives during the war, making sure that this important facility did not fall into rogue hands. Soon the Americans would be retreating from Czechoslovakia, leaving the territory to the Russians. But in the meantime, Reed was required to keep boots on the ground and guns loaded until the Third Army—the 2nd Cavalry included—was ordered to retreat.

For Reed and his men, nothing could diminish what they had accomplished in rescuing these four-footed beauties. All of the horses were safe in American territory, not a single one hurt on the ride. Back in 1942, when Reed had taken command of the 2nd Cavalry, it had seemed that the force's days of equestrian valor were behind them forever. But today, the regiment had earned a place among its honored horseback-riding predecessors.

24.

THE LIPIZZANER FAREWELL

Kötzting, Bavaria, Germany, May 16–21, 1945

For the first time in his life, Alois Podhajsky was flying—high in the sky in General Collier's military airplane en route to 2nd Cavalry headquarters at the Skoda Castle, in Czechoslovakia. The Austrian was on his way to meet the man who had saved his Lipizzaners: Colonel Hank Reed. Podhajsky's mission was to pick out his mares and foals for transport back to Austria. *Are they safe and healthy?* he wondered. *Have any been lost?*

When the small plane landed on the castle's vast grounds, an American major led Podhajsky into the opulent building, through a maze of hallways, and finally to a comfortable bedroom, where he was told to make himself at home. The commander of the 2nd Cavalry, Colonel Reed, would join him for dinner. At six p.m., the major returned and escorted him to meet the colonel.

Immediately, the colonel's warm smile set the Austrian at ease. During dinner, the two men discussed their favorite

subject—horses. Reed told Podhajsky that he had recognized
the Austrian's name from the 1936 Olympics. In fact, a Fort
Riley cavalryman had named one of the school's horses after
him—they called him Podhorski.

Reed filled Podhajsky in on what had happened over the
last two weeks. The Americans, he explained, had captured the
stud farm intact, but the farm lay in territory that now belonged
to the Russians. Fearing that the Americans would soon pull
back and the Russians would seize the horses or the Czechoslo-
vakians would claim them as Czech property, Reed had made
the difficult decision to move them to the village of Kötzting,
Germany. Fortunately, the horses had arrived safely, but conditions were dangerous—he wanted to return the Lipizzaners to
Austria as soon as possible.

Podhajsky explained to Reed that there was just one hitch.
Not all of the Lipizzaners in Hostau were *from* Austria—some
had been brought there from the stud farm in Lipica, Italy;
others had come from the royal Lipizzaner stud of Yugoslavia;
still more had been brought from other locations. Reed was
alarmed to hear of this unexpected complication, having anticipated that all of the Lipizzaners would be returned to Vienna.

The next morning, Reed and Podhajsky set out for Kötzting in Reed's jeep through the Czechoslovakian countryside;
Reed's men reported that the horses had arrived safely, but he
could not vouch for their condition since. As they approached,
Podhajsky was nervous, fearing the worst.

Hours later, they were greeted by Lessing, who was over-
worked and tired, but eager to welcome his former colleague.
Lessing and Podhajsky had met the previous year, when the

Austrian visited Hostau to check on his mares. Their relationship had been cordial as the two had discussed the horses' welfare over coffee in the veterinarian's home.

Though Lessing still considered the Austrian his friend,
he was surprised that Podhajsky refused to shake his hand or
look him in the eye. Lessing was hurt by the treatment—they
had shared a love of horses, and both had worn the Wehrmacht
uniform. But their common past could no longer overcome the
politics that had come between them: Lessing was a defeated
German, Podhajsky was a liberated Austrian; the veterinarian
was an American POW, and the director of the Spanish Riding School was a free man. Their circumstances were entirely
different.

As Reed, Lessing, and Podhajsky toured the stables, Podhajsky instantly recognized the mares from Piber, calling out to
them by name. The white horses looked up and whinnied when
they saw the familiar face. Podhajsky walked among them, easily picking out the ones branded with a P and a crown over it.
There were 219 Austrian mares in all. Forty or so Lipizzaners
that did not come from Austria had been brought to Hostau
from Yugoslavia and Italy, and some had been foaled at Hostau,
but Podhajsky pointed out that each horse's provenance could
be readily determined by its brands.

Hank Reed knew that courts and tribunals would decide
where these horses should end up. For now, he just needed to
get them out of Kötzting. He asked Podhajsky to return the
purebred Lipizzaners—including those from Lipica and from
the royal Yugoslavian stud farm—to Austria for safekeeping
until their proper final destination could be sorted out.

Podhajsky reflected on the situation in St. Martin. Already, he had trouble caring for his seventy stallions. Could he really agree to take so many more horses and be responsible for them? He hesitated only a minute before agreeing to find temporary homes for the Lipizzaners from Lipica and from the royal Yugoslavian stud farm. This would leave behind about fifteen Lipizzaners with the Americans, those gathered from entirely different countries. The following day, Podhajsky returned to St. Martin. The horses would arrive within a week.

On May 22, Quinlivan and Lessing prepared to load the Lipizzaners onto the forty trucks that would transport them to Podhajsky's home base at the Arco Castle in St. Martin, Austria. What was left of the group of captured horses— including the Arabians from Janów Podlaski and the remaining Lipizzaners—would soon be sent to another captured German stud farm. Witez had survived his long journey in remarkably good condition. His mane was silken, his eyes bright, his spirited expression undampened. The stallion's fate remained in the hands of the 2nd Cavalry.

Each truck would transport about fifteen of the 219 mares and foals; the rest carried POWs to act as grooms, as well as food and supplies for the horses.

Ever since the Germans had taken the mares out of Austria, Podhajsky had wondered if they would ever return. Now, the Lipizzaner mares would be reunited with their home country.

A difficult new path lay ahead of him. Yes, he had the horses, and yes, Reed and Patton had fulfilled their promises.

But now more than three hundred mares and stallions were counting on him—a worn-out forty-seven-year-old citizen of a defeated nation—to keep them safe. The country of Austria would need to reinvent itself, and the Spanish Riding School too would need to find a new path to assure its future.

PART FOUR

Homecoming

25.

THE SUPER HORSES ARE OURS

The war was over, but the scheming and fighting over Germany's purebred horses had just begun. During the past six years, Hitler had systematically seized Europe's finest equine specimens. Now these four-footed treasures were among the most valuable assets captured by the Americans.

By late May 1945, Germany was jammed with pedigreed horses. Some of these had been seized from occupied countries by Rau and his men. Others had been lucky enough to avoid the Russians, survive the hardships of the trek, and make it across the German border. All of them required food and shelter.

The American army, exhausted after its long fight through Europe, now had the task of trying to reestablish a functioning government, ensure basic services for citizens, discharge German prisoners of war, *and* sort through a vast muddle of displaced people and property. Among all of these demands, sorting out the fate of the horses was a minor one. Until a resolution was found, though, these animals needed immediate care and attention.

In Kötzting, Reed had an urgent situation on his hands. The horses from Hostau would soon run out of feed. Even after 219 Lipizzaners had been returned to Podhajsky in Austria, more than a hundred rescued purebreds remained with nowhere to go. Reed knew that these horses were Polish, Yugoslavian, and Russian in origin, but no one could explain precisely *how* they had ended up in Hostau; nor did anyone seem to have authority to negotiate a return to their rightful owners—if such owners could be found. Hoping to prevent the horses from being sold off, he tried to find uses for them, distributing those that were suitable for everyday riding to officers, and even sending five mounts to General Patton. Still, more than ninety horses remained, including the Arabians from Poland, Witez and Lotnik.

Eager to get the horses safely out of Kötzting, Reed next sent them to Mansbach, a captured German stud farm. There, Quinlivan, Lessing, and Kroll found well-appointed stables with roomy box stalls and green pastures. For the first time since leaving Hostau, the horses could graze and stretch their legs. However, finding adequate food was still a problem. Witez and the other rescues were no longer in immediate danger, but Reed knew that if given the order, he would have to take his men off the task of looking after the horses—and then how would the horses survive?

The next order of business was to determine whether the seizure of the horses from Czechoslovakia had been legal. On June 16 and 17, Reed, Tom Stewart, and Hubert Rudofsky were called to Third Army headquarters to testify in front of the inspector general, Clarence C. Cook. The men swore under oath that the horses' pedigrees were accurate and that none of them belonged to Czechoslovakia—they had been moved there from elsewhere for safekeeping. Cook concluded that the horses' capture was lawful and that the purebreds could be claimed by the Americans as spoils of war.

Now that the horses *officially* belonged to the U.S. Army, the question of what to do with them remained. A stroke of good fortune occurred for the horses when, in early August 1945, Colonel Fred Hamilton was appointed chief of the army's Remount Service. Hamilton was a passionate horse lover with a firm belief in continuing the army's role in breeding horses. He was about to be presented with a once-in-a-lifetime opportunity.

In spring 1945, Colonel Hamilton visited the stud farm at Mansbach. He was impressed by the magnificent Polish Arabians that Reed and his men had captured—but he was unsure *where* these horses belonged. He knew little of the tragic true story of the Arabians from Janów Podlaski. Had Hamilton known the full story, he would have realized that there were Polish citizens who cared greatly for these horses and were hoping to return them to their native land.

But Hamilton knew only what he had learned from the horses' German captors—people who, it later became clear, were eager to cover up their role in Poland during the war. Added to this misinformation was the Americans' suspicions of Russia's intentions, and their belief that those claiming to act on behalf of Poland or Yugoslavia were actually puppets of the Bolsheviks hoping to seize the horses to build up the Soviet military.

Fred Hamilton decided that the best of the horses should be shipped to America to be bred and cared for. In his official report, he wrote, "If the US does not acquire shipment of this breeding stock, in the near future it will be completely lost to the horse world. The Europeans are not in a position to maintain stock; [they] must sell some of it, and certain nations to the east are eager to acquire it by any means, legal or otherwise." In his mind, these horses had value for the military, and even advances in technology—from cars to atomic bombs—didn't change that.

But Europe was teeming with American soldiers eager to return home. Their equipment needed shipment as well. Could Hamilton possibly convince the War Department to commit precious manpower and space to *horses*?

In Mansbach, the summer of 1945 passed peacefully for the men and horses. Lieutenant Quinlivan and veterinarian Rudolf Lessing had become friends, riding together every day. Caring for the refined horses was not easy, though. People were scrounging to get by, never knowing in the morning where their dinner would come from, much less how to feed their animals. Lessing not only looked after the horses under the care of the 2nd Cavalry; he also made rounds in the surrounding countryside in his car, looking after the animals of impoverished local farmers. He kept a milk pail in his car so he could ask to be paid in fresh milk if a farmer had no cash.

Lessing dreamed of a future when people could once again ride horses for pleasure and sport, but every day presented so many challenges that it was hard to imagine when that time would come. For this reason, he supported the idea of passing the remaining horses to the Americans. He couldn't see any other safe way forward for them. Witez, in his stable, seemed settled enough, but no decision had been made about his ultimate fate. It was becoming increasingly clear that if Colonel Fred Hamilton couldn't find a way to ship the horses to the United States, the army could not be responsible for their care much longer. And then what would happen to them?

As the summer of 1945 drew to a close, Reed passed his responsibility for the horses on to Colonel Hamilton. Patton had put Reed in charge of the force patrolling the tense border region of Germany; one of Reed's first actions was to mount some of the MPs on horseback. He had plenty of work but more opportunity to relax than before. His carriage, pulled by a pair of Lipizzaner coach horses, was a familiar sight around his new headquarters near Munich. After so many long, lonely months at war, Reed's wife, Janice, had joined him in Germany. But the last few months had also seen a stream of deeply felt farewells: The men of the 2nd Cavalry had grown so close that some felt like members of his own family—none more so than the faithful young man who had saved his life numerous times, Jim O'Leary. Hank wrote a letter to the young man's mother back in Chicago. In it, he said, "I have no sons. Had I one, I could wish nothing more but that he be a son as fine as yours."

On September 1, Tom Stewart prepared for his return to the United States. In May, Stewart had been awarded the Bronze Star for bravery, honoring his mission to Hostau. But he did not consider himself a hero. The memories of his comrades lost in the fields had affected him profoundly, deepening his natural reserve. Witez, with his velvety nose and proud expression, helped remind Stewart of the good he had accomplished. Almost two years after sailing from New York Harbor aboard the *Mauretania,* Tom Stewart was heading home at last, knowing he had done everything he could do on behalf of the horses.

After Tom Stewart's departure, the only remaining member of the 2nd Cavalry still with the horses was Lieutenant Quinlivan. On September 19, 1945, he received top secret orders from the War Department: He and Colonel Fred Hamilton, along with another cavalry officer and two veterinarians, now formed the special delegation team known as "the horse detectives." Their mission? To select the best of the captured horses for shipment to America.

For the next three weeks, "the horse detectives" toured the four captured German stud farms and examined the top-flight show horses belonging to the German Army equestrian team. At each stop, the team evaluated the horses' conformation, temperament, performance, and pedigrees. They scrutinized sketchy records that claimed to show German ownership of horses seized from other countries. The horse detectives would not take any horse back to America with them whose private ownership or unlawful seizure could be determined.

Throughout the summer, a stream of visitors came to Mansbach—including Gustav Rau. Rau had ridden out the war at a German remount depot in northern Germany. His role during wartime in the stud farm administration of Poland would be largely swept under the rug. Sadly, in later years, as the Polish government tried to get back the horses the Germans had seized from them, Gustav Rau would become the chief source of misinformation about them—dashing any hope that the seized Arabians from Hostau would ever be returned to their homeland.

By the end of September, Hamilton and his fellow horse detectives had selected 150 horses, including the Lipizzaner mare Madera, the refined gray Arabian Lotnik, and the 2nd Cavalry favorite, the beloved Witez. By his own account, Hamilton had strived to select horses most suitable for the army's breeding program. For the time being, Hamilton felt confident that he had picked the very best horses for the benefit of the horses, the army, and by extension, the American people.

Reed made a final visit to the stables at Mansbach. Pleased with the two Germans' loyalty and skilled work, Reed had invited Lessing and Kroll to join the horses on the trip to America, where the veterinarians would have a chance to start a new life. Kroll agreed to the offer. Lessing decided to stay with his family and let the Americans and his beloved horses leave without him.

In honor of his efforts, Hank Reed presented Lessing with a letter of commendation, praising him for his outstanding service. For Reed, Lessing and Kroll had prepared a leather-bound photo album full of pictures of the horses. A majestic photograph of the Lipizzaner stallion Neapolitano Slavonia graced the cover. Hank Reed slowly turned the pages, looking through the photos of the foals, mares, riding horses, and stallions. One of the captions read "The Lipizzaner galloping across the field at sunset, like something out of a fairytale . . ."

Politics, prejudice, and intolerance had riven a brutal divide between the countries of these men; the grace of these horses had started to bring them together. The former enemies parted as friends.

26.

DEPARTURE!

Bremerhaven, Germany, October 1, 1945

Out on the busy docks at Bremerhaven, among the battered ship containers, sturdy white Lipizzaners, slender blue-blooded Thoroughbreds, high-crested Arabians, and a single Cossack horse circled nervously, tugging on the lead ropes held tightly by uniformed American soldiers.

Soon they would board the Liberty ship *Stephen F. Austin*. Down in the hold, the crew had built makeshift individual box stalls for the stallions. The mares were placed in narrow standing stalls, and the foals were grouped in small pens. As the horsemen settled the horses into their quarters, up on deck, the jubilant soldiers leaned against the ship's railings with grins on their faces. They had anticipated this day since the moment they'd set foot on this continent back in the summer of 1944. At long last, they were headed home.

From the 2nd Cavalry, only Quin Quinlivan would accompany the horses on their transatlantic crossing. Joining him was German veterinarian Wolfgang Kroll. One of the Arabian mares, Gospa, had foaled during the rail journey to the docks. The men had opened her boxcar in the morning to see a tiny Arabian peering out from her mother's side. Most wonderful of all was the telltale misshapen star on her forehead. This little filly would be Witez's first offspring to grow up in America.

Rudolf Lessing accompanied the group to the dock to say goodbye. Watching the horses depart was bittersweet. He knew that when the ship and crew embarked, he would return home empty-handed. The mission he had started the previous April, when he had ridden across the border into Germany, had at last come to an end. From here on out, the fate of the horses rested with the American army. When the last of the horses had departed for distant shores, Rudolf Lessing turned around and went home to his wife and children, and to his dawn-to-dusk routine of helping animals in need.

Spirits were high as the *Stephen F. Austin* pulled out of the port of Bremerhaven on October 12, 1945. Sailing along the coast of Holland, they could see windmills in the distance, and the seas were calm. But the soldiers were edgy—these waters were laced with lethal undetonated mines. Each man breathed a sigh of relief when at last they sailed out of the dangerous corridor without mishap. Down below, Quinlivan made sure the horses were fed and watered. In the best of circumstances, with ample exercise and fresh air, stallions can be a handful. Here in the hold of the ship, the horses would be cooped up for the entire crossing, which was expected to last about twelve days. Keeping them calm would be a big job. Still, the sun was shining, and all aboard were hoping for a peaceful trip. It was hard to believe, but in just a few days, these horses would be safe in America.

Five days into the journey, as they entered the Bay of Biscay, the seas got heavier. The ship started to roll. At first, the horses seemed better off than the men in the rough seas. The four-legged animals could balance even when the men were hardly able to stand. Quinlivan and the team hovered around the horses, making sure they were all right. But as the storm worsened, even the horses began to wobble. Belowdecks, it felt like a roller coaster. Only Witez, as balanced as a cat, shifted but never seemed to panic. When Quinlivan approached him, he blew a puff of warm breath across the soldier's cheek, as if to say, "Don't worry about me."

The weather grew worse. Winds whipped across the decks at seventy-five miles an hour, and the ship was making no headway. At the helm, the captain's compass wasn't working; he was struggling to navigate. Hoping to find the shortest route to the other side, he decided to head the ship directly into the storm. But as soon as he did, the vessel started pitching dangerously from side to side.

In the cargo hold, the lights had blown out and it was pitch-dark. Quinlivan could hear the bone-chilling sounds of stallions screaming, hooves clanging against metal and boards, and mares whinnying. Each time the ship rolled, the horses were flung back and forth against the wooden planks that separated them. When a particularly giant wave sent the ship almost horizontal, the planks separating the horses finally splintered. The horses were thrown out into the hold.

Quinlivan bolted into action to save them. With just the light of a single lantern, he climbed into the midst of the fray; the rest of the men followed close behind him.

In the small pool of light afforded by the lantern, they shuddered at what they saw. The force of the storm had knocked the horses clear of their enclosures and piled the priceless stallions in a heap. They were fighting and kicking one another in a flashing tangle of bared teeth, sharp hooves, and flaring nostrils in the dark. The mares had been thrown from their enclosures as well. The terrified horses were just as dangerous to the men as the bullets they had so recently escaped.

Still, Quinlivan's men thought nothing of their own safety. Pushing away any thought of fear, they moved into the tangle, trying frantically to separate the animals before they killed one another. All of the miles traversed, all of the danger faced, all of the lives risked and even lost to save these horses—all of it was on the verge of being wasted.

Quinlivan set about looking for Gospa's foal, fearing the worst—just a few days old, the tiny foal could easily be killed by the flailing hooves of a furious stallion. Miraculously, she was unscathed: Gospa had managed to stand guard, shielding her precious charge with her body. Next, Quinlivan made his way to Witez. Even in the chaos, Witez seemed to understand that panicking would only make matters worse. Quinlivan stroked the horse's nose for a moment, whispering a quiet word of thanks. Witez, the chieftain, had been bred to maintain his composure in the fury of battle—and here on the *Stephen F. Austin*, he had won his warrior's stripes.

By the time the men got the horses separated, many of the animals were injured. The veterinarians squatted on the straw floor, improvised sterile fields laid out in front of them, and sutured up the horses' wounds with steady hands while men held flashlights to illuminate the work.

Finally, after hours of constant attention, the animals were sewn up and bandaged and their makeshift stalls were rebuilt. The horses were spent. The men were so exhausted that they could hardly stand. But all of them were going to survive.

The seas slowly calmed. The ocean had turned to a tranquil turquoise filigreed with seaweed; Quinlivan knew that the serene seas did not spell the end of their troubles. The captain's detour around the storm had thrown them off course. The crossing, which was originally supposed to take around twelve days, had been extended to over two weeks. Safely on the other side of the tempest, the horsemen faced a different sort of emergency—their stores of hay and grain were running dangerously low. Two days before reaching port, they ran out of feed. If the trip had lasted any longer, some of the horses might not have survived.

On October 28, 1945, the *Stephen F. Austin* and its exhausted cargo of men and beasts pulled up to the dock in Newport News, Virginia. Sixteen days on the high seas, through a battering storm, with inadequate feed, had left the horses looking weary and battle-worn—their cuts and nicks not yet healed, their coats dull, and their bodies thin—but they had made it.

27.

THE RIDERLESS HORSE

Luxembourg, December 22, 1945

Six months had passed since the raid on Hostau; in a surprising twist of fate, the rescued horses were safely settled in Hank Reed's native Virginia while he remained in Germany.

Then, on December 9, 1945, a piece of gloomy news spread like wildfire. General George S. Patton had been seriously injured in a car accident in the Rhineland. Like everyone in Europe and America, Hank Reed was shocked to hear the news. Patton had suffered a fractured spine and was paralyzed from the neck down. When his doctor came to talk to him, Patton, the ultimate cavalryman, had only one question: "Will I ever ride again?"

During the months before Patton's accident, emotions had been running high on a subject that mattered deeply to both Patton and Reed: the role of horses in the army after World War II. With only a few exceptions, no American horses had been used in combat during the hostilities. Nevertheless, the role of the horse in the army—including the riding school at

Fort Riley and the prestigious equestrian events—were so central to the force's history that many could not imagine the army without them. Patton had been drawn into the debate. He wrote to his friend General Jacob Devers, head of Army Ground Forces in Washington, pleading with him to retain a role for horses.

More than any other individual, Patton had been instrumental in drumming up support for the captured horses that had safely landed in America, but he did not live long enough to see what became of them. Thirteen days after his automobile accident, George Patton died at age sixty of a pulmonary embolism. According to the wishes he had expressed to his wife, Beatrice, he was to be buried alongside his men at the American Military Cemetery in Luxembourg.

Hank Reed had a final service to perform in Patton's honor. It was his duty to organize the color guard and the horses at what would be one of the most watched military funerals in modern history. The day of Patton's funeral was dark, with a cold, steady drizzle falling on the mourners. Reed had attended to every single detail, carefully preparing the black horse that would follow the casket through the streets of Luxembourg City, a city liberated by the Americans only a year earlier.

Heads of state and high-ranking military officers followed as the flag-draped coffin passed through the cobblestone streets of the somber, wintry city. Patton's widow followed the coffin in the first car. Massive armored cars and powerful tanks rolled along in formation, showcasing the technological might of the United States Army. As the coffin passed, mourners removed their hats to pay respect to the great leader.

A caparisoned horse followed Patton's coffin in the procession. The black horse wore Patton's saddle, draped with black crepe. The general's high boots were placed in the stirrups, their toes facing backward. The silent dignity of the riderless horse symbolized this tragic loss.

With the victorious general's death, it seemed that the end of an era had come. The man who had, during the 1912 Olympics, run, swum, fenced, shot at a target, and jumped a horse to demonstrate his fitness as a soldier, had departed a world that had changed almost beyond recognition during his lifetime. Hank Reed and the men of the cavalry had lost a friend, a leader, and the army's most passionate defender of horses.

28.

THE VICTORY PARADE

Front Royal, Virginia, April 7, 1946

Soft sunshine beamed down on the kelly-green pastures surrounding the Aleshire Army Remount Depot in Front Royal,
Virginia. The war was over, the Allies had won, and the equestrian world was abuzz with the news that the army had not *only*
removed the Nazis from power but had also made off with a
king's ransom of horses. Now a parade was being held to intro-
duce these horses to America.

His face shaded by a broad-brimmed campaign hat, Captain Quinlivan passed quietly among his four-footed friends,
whispering soothing words. The horses responded with soft
whinnies and friendly nudges, pleased to see a familiar face
among the throngs of strangers.

For months since their arrival, the European imports had
been sheltered from view. Today the public would see these
spectacular purebreds for the first time. The event had drawn a
large crowd of interested spectators, as well as a gaggle of jour-
nalists from the local and national press corps. They all chat-

tered in excited tones while they perused the exotic names and pedigrees of the horses.

In the year following the end of the war, stories about captured horses continued to seize headlines. The horses' arrival had not been free from controversy, though. Drew Pearson, a columnist for the *Washington Post*, had issued a public scolding, implying that the animals had used up precious ship space at the expense of American soldiers who were still awaiting their chance to ship home.

Others argued that the German horses' blood might taint that of the American-breds—an argument that held traces of the old eugenicist theories that had driven Gustav Rau's breeding enterprise. The Americans had gained control of these horses by defeating Nazi Germany; now, ironically, Nazi-style arguments related to the purity of their blood were being marshaled against them.

Colonel Fred Hamilton had painstakingly cleared the horses and checked their pedigrees before taking them from Germany. He had even flown home to be the first to greet them in America. Now he was frustrated, for it seemed that his rescued animals would not be judged on speed and skill alone. If the horses could not be registered in America's breeding program, their value to the American horse-racing industry—which allowed only Thoroughbreds with registered bloodlines to compete— would be destroyed.

Until this day, no one in America outside a select group of cavalrymen had actually laid eyes on these much-talked-about horses. The animals were bound to make a stunning impression. Lotnik's pearlescent coat gleamed. Witez, the chieftain, shone bright as flame.

At two p.m., in the large outdoor arena of the Front Royal complex, it was time for the parade to begin. Clustered at ringside, people jostled while eagerly flipping through their programs. A hush fell over the crowd as cavalrymen began to lead the slender, light-footed Thoroughbreds, one by one, across the viewing area. The assembled horsemen nodded and murmured in appreciation as Quinlivan noted their response to Witez, his favorite, with satisfaction. Even among an extraordinary collection of horseflesh, this genuine descendant of a pure-blooded desert-bred Arabian was a one-of-a-kind beauty.

The final event of the parade of horses was a driving display by four Lipizzaner mares pulling an imperial coach. Most of the people in the stands were completely unfamiliar with the Lipizzaner breed. Alongside the lanky Thoroughbreds, the white horses looked stocky and compact, their Roman noses, a sign of their elegant breeding, unappealing to American taste. Nor did the audience know anything of the intricate dressage moves and leaps that had made these horses so famous in Europe. A cavalry lieutenant drove the four-in-hand with panache, and the audience was impressed at the novel sight—but even so, the Lipizzaner were unable to seize the spectators' interest like the more familiar Thoroughbreds.

Certainly, there would have been eager prospective buyers for many of the rescued horses among the well-heeled crowd assembled to see them on parade, but these refugees were not for sale. The rescued horses remained the property of the United States Army. In April 1946, Colonel Hamilton's Remount Service was still operating five major horse-breeding operations in addition to the one in Front Royal. Hamilton's plan was to disperse the horses among the different depots. Only the

Thoroughbreds would remain at Front Royal. Quinlivan had been reassigned to Fort Robinson, Nebraska, and Witez was being shipped to Pomona, California. After spending almost a year together, the friends had their marching orders: They were going separate ways.

29.

FINDING A HOME

A year had passed since Podhajsky and his stallions had fled the elegant Spanish Riding School. For now, a return to Vienna so soon after the war remained impossible. Peace had brought stability to Austria, but the country remained under Allied occupation, divided into sectors controlled by the United States, Great Britain, France, and the Soviet Union. Vienna was likewise divided, although its center was now a shared international zone.

Thanks to Patton's decree in 1945, the Lipizzaners and the Spanish Riding School had been granted American protection. Their safety and ongoing support were assured as long as they remained within the American zone. But the Imperial Stables stood empty. Podhajsky's dream of returning the horses to their school had not dimmed, but in the meantime the Lipizzaners would be relocated to Wels, Austria. Wels was where he, as a young man, had started his career as a cavalry soldier. Here, with adequate stabling and a large riding hall, he hoped that the horses could gradually reestablish a state of normalcy and routine.

By April 1946, the move was complete. Stallions and mares settled in their new quarters. For the first time since leaving Vienna with the horses, Podhajsky could free his mind from questions of daily survival. He still had no money, no support, and no real long-term plan. Podhajsky knew the prewar world was gone, and with it the infrastructure that had supported the school. He needed to invent a new future for the horses.

Halfway across the globe, in Pomona, California, Witez cantered along a hillside trail, kicking up small puffs of dust with each stride. His coat shone with a coppery fire; his black tail floated behind him like plumes of blowing smoke. On his back, his groom and rider, Joe Benes, was riding Western-style, holding braided leather reins in one hand. Citrus groves and ornamental rose gardens spread out below them. Behind them soared the snowcapped San Gabriel Mountains. After traveling halfway across the globe, the Arabian stallion appeared to have landed in paradise.

In 1946, when Witez arrived in Pomona, he was stabled in one of the finest Arabian horse-breeding establishments in the world. The Pomona Remount Depot, where Witez now lived, was the jewel in the army's crown. A million-dollar property (in 1940s dollars), it was the former home of W. K. Kellogg, one of the world's foremost breeders of purebred Arabian horses. Even among these celebrity Arabians, the Polish chieftain immediately attracted attention. The Remount Service offered him at stud; Witez quickly proved his strength as a father to many local foals. One local rancher wanted desperately to buy him. But the horses belonged to the Quartermaster Corps and were not for sale.

Despite his success as a remount stallion, Witez's future remained in question; the army's commitment to horse breeding was wavering. With the passing of Patton in 1945, the horse had lost its most powerful ally. In Washington, Colonel Fred Hamilton continued to plead on behalf of the Remount Service. But privately, Hamilton was feeling hopeless. As if the storm at sea on the *Stephen F. Austin* had been a sign of things to come, the horses had faced nothing but problems since their arrival.

The head of Pomona's Army Remount Depot, Colonel F. W. Koester, had been a persistent advocate for the Arabians during his tenure. In 1946 and 1947, Koester fought for the animals' pedigrees to be authenticated so the horses could be registered. If they were not, they would lose all of their value for breeding. But American breeding organizations continued to voice skepticism about authenticating the bloodlines of horses seized in wartime.

As the one soldier who had been with the horses at each step of their transfer from Hostau to the United States, Quinlivan gave a sworn affidavit as to the horses' identities and the manner of their capture, and as to the trustworthiness of the Germans— Lessing and Rudofsky—who had vouched for the authenticity of their pedigrees. Through the efforts of Colonel Koester, both Witez and Lotnik were eventually registered with the Arabian Horse Registry of America, assuring their continuing value as sires. But Colonel Koester was set to retire at the end of 1947, leaving no one else to advocate for the horses.

Additionally, several European countries—Hungary, Poland, and Yugoslavia—had filed suits claiming that their horses
had been seized unlawfully. In response, the Senate Armed Services Committee recommended that the horses be returned to
their countries of origin. In a sudden reversal, the committee
then blocked the decision and ruled that the horses were America's legitimate spoils of war. The wrangling over the rescued
horses' fate did not solve one important underlying problem:
Two years after the end of a horseless war, no one had been able
to make a convincing argument that the army should continue
to breed them.

30.

THE WAR ORPHANS

Pomona, California, December 1, 1948

As 1948 drew to a close, three years after the war had been won at the cost of more than four hundred thousand American lives, the men of the 2nd Cavalry were scattered across America. Eagerly, they picked up the pieces of the lives they had left behind during the war years. Some, like Captain Quinlivan, were still in the army; others, like Tom Stewart, had been discharged and were trying to find their footing in the civilian world. Many of them had cut out newspaper and magazine articles about the horses' triumphant arrival in Newport News, but as the years passed, the men lost track of the horses. The memory of the wartime rescue was tucked away with the rest of their war souvenirs.

By this time, the 231 horses imported to America by the horse detectives had met a variety of fates. Support for the Remount Service dwindled, and by late 1946, Fred Hamilton had been required to auction off most of the Thoroughbreds at Front Royal. His promise of the Thoroughbreds' great value was not borne out. The refusal of the American Jockey Club to register the Thoroughbreds had greatly diminished their worth. Without registration papers, the majority of these horses' descendants could not be traced, significantly limiting their value. As a result, most of the horses that had been captured to such great fanfare just a few years earlier had mostly gone on to ordinary lives on private farms, parks, or estates.

The army cavalry had a last hurrah when it cobbled together an equestrian team to ride in the 1948 Olympics in London. In November of that year, the Army Equestrian Team made its final public appearance at the National Horse Show in Madison Square Garden. When members of the Dutch team spotted a couple of their own horses in the American stables, the army handed them back to their rightful owners. Meanwhile, cavalry veterans were offered a chance to purchase army horses at a discount. Many took advantage of the offer to buy strings of horses and establish riding academies. The future of equestrian sports from here on in would be civilian. Still, a few of the horses from Hostau, including Witez and Lotnik, remained with the Remount Service, their destiny uncertain, their plight unknown to the men who had rescued them.

On July 1, 1948, the Defense Department, under the order of President Harry Truman, formally transferred its remaining Remount Depots with all of their livestock and equipment to the Department of Agriculture. With lightning speed, horse lovers' hopes were dashed. The Agriculture Department declared that its budget would not support any horse-breeding operations. The department planned to sell off all remaining animals immediately.

The number of horses in the army had already dropped

dramatically, from the more than 200,000 horses in 1941 to just 327 in 1949. At Fort Riley, the soldiers lovingly cared for some of the distinguished retired horses from the army's competitive equestrian days. At the Pomona Remount Depot, only Kellogg's prized Arabians, the imports from Janów Podlaski, and nine Lipizzaners remained.

Witez had lived through the bombings of wartime, but now, in his peaceful home, a new sort of battle ensued. As soon as the Department of Agriculture assumed control of the Pomona Remount Depot, their staff began a ruthless process of selection, culling the Arabian herd. Many of the able-bodied animals were sold off. Older mares and stallions, past their prime for breeding, were targeted for euthanization. Only the cream of the crop remained.

Arabian-horse lovers, horrified by this callous treatment, started rescue operations, determined to save as many of the beautiful animals as possible. Sometimes they succeeded. But by the fall of 1948, only the most valuable horses in the Kellogg stables remained. Among these was Witez. In October 1948, even these finest horses were to be sold off at auction, until this announcement faced a backlash from horse organizations and animal rights petitioners.

The Department of Agriculture changed its approach. Rather than auction the remaining animals, the department announced its decision to move them to Fort Reno, Oklahoma, where the horse-breeding operations had not yet been fully curtailed. Many assumed that this announcement was a lie, and that the horses would be quietly sold. One thing was clear: The United States government was not in the horse business any longer, and these animals, products of the most refined pedigrees in the world, were suddenly about as valuable to them as a bunch of worn tires from an old-model jeep.

On December 1, 1948, the Pomona ranch appeared serene as a line of horses paraded toward a waiting railcar. The Arabians stepped lightly across the dusty train yard, seeming too regal for these ordinary surroundings. The mild California sunshine shone upon their fine coats, bringing out the copper, silver, and gold. A gaggle of reporters and press photographers had gathered to witness their dispersal.

Four mares with foals at their sides were loaded into the train first, then four yearling stallions, one six-year-old, one ten-year old, and a pure white Lipizzaner coach horse.

At the very back of the line, last to load, stood Witez. With his large, dark eyes, he paused, looking at the assembled crowd like a monarch surveying his subjects. As cameras flashed, the stallion flicked his curved ears forward, their delicate tips pointing inward. The chieftain entered the shadowy boxcar without looking back.

After Witez was settled in the train, his handler, Joe Benes, offered him a sugar lump, then planted a kiss on the animal's soft muzzle, lingering an extra moment at his side. But the train's engine was revving, and Benes, who had been caring for this stallion and riding him daily since his arrival from Front Royal in 1946, had no choice but to unclasp the lead rope and walk away.

Had anyone noticed, as he boarded the train, the brand just behind the stallion's left shoulder? Witez still wore the mark of his birthplace in Poland: a royal crown. But that had not protected this knight, this chieftain, this warrior. This train to nowhere rattled east all the same.

At the end of 1947, Colonel Fred Hamilton, who had worked so hard to bring the captured horses to the United States, had retired from the army on disability at the age of fifty-one. Publicly, he remained an outspoken advocate for horses. Privately, he had started calling these last remaining horses "the war orphans."

31.

THE AUCTION

Fort Reno, Oklahoma, Spring 1949

In the spring of 1949, Witez was in his prime, glowing with health and vitality. But the eleven-year-old Polish chieftain, the stolen treasure of the Third Reich, was a precious jewel in a tarnished setting—especially today, May 25, when he stood in a dusty corral with the number 131 pasted on his hip.

Just a few short months after Witez arrived in Fort Reno, Oklahoma, the Department of Agriculture sneakily changed its mind: It *would*, after all, close down the last of the army's remount program and sell off the remaining horses.

The auction of exotic Arabians and Lipizzaners had attracted a motley assortment of buyers. A movie company, a circus, and a variety of local ranchers had gathered to bid on these formerly priceless horses; news of the sale was not widely publicized, so those most aware of the horses' true value had not heard of the impending sale.

Witez couldn't have looked more out of place. Of all the destinations on his long journey, this one, ending on the dusty plains of Fort Reno, was the most desolate. Witez had arrived without a single familiar face to greet him. No one knew this glorious stallion's extraordinary story.

However, it turned out that one of the veterans of the 2nd Cavalry was in Fort Reno on the day of this terminal sale. Shortly before the auction started, a slight, dark-haired man moved quietly past the corrals where the horses were lined up, ready to enter the showground. The man's step was soft but purposeful. He was looking for an old friend, a companion he had once loved and watched over. He passed through the crowd of elegant horses, almost without looking; there was only one he wanted to see.

The veteran first heard the deep, full-throated whinny and then saw the face—the dark eyes set off by an irregular white star, the curved ears that seemed almost to touch when they were pricked forward. The man leaned up against the wooden fence, and the stallion approached. The Arabian extended his nose. His nostrils fluted. Joyfully, Captain Tom Stewart put out his hand.

Stewart, the man whose midnight ride had set the stage for the rescue of the horses from Hostau, had not seen any of them since September 1945. He had been honored for his bravery in the raid, yet after a few months at home in Bethesda, like many veterans, he had found the transition to civilian life difficult. Still haunted by the friends he had lost and the brutality he had witnessed, he had trouble fitting into the social whirl afforded a senator's son. A few months after returning home, he set off on a cross-country journey, hitchhiking across the American West, stopping to work as a day laborer pumping gas or washing cars when he needed money. As if guided by a divine hand, his journey had brought him here to Fort Reno to see his old friend Witez for the last time. Stewart was in no position to buy Witez—standing there at the dusty ringside, he could only hope that this horse, for which much had been sacrificed, would find a loving home.

At ten a.m., the auction began. When the auctioneer called out, "One-thirty-one," Witez raised his head, his forelock rakishly sweeping across the white star on his forehead. He pranced forward, holding his black tail proudly aloft. Prospective buyers studied the program, a typescript pamphlet of a few pages with just the barest information: *Hip # 131, a bay stallion, foaled in 1938, 15 hands, son of Ofir and Federajca. Certified by the Arabian Horse Club No. 3933.* That was it.

Nowhere in the brochure did it tell of a frightened young groom daubing mud on the colt's sides, hoping to escape notice from the advancing Russians. Nowhere did it mention boarding a train to Czechoslovakia, or parading on a muddy field in front of a group of Nazi grandees. Nor did it mention a gentle-handed veterinarian, Rudolf Lessing, who had risked his life to try to save this horse. No mention was made of Tom Stewart, the soft-voiced captain who had accompanied Lessing under cover of darkness to secure his surrender. Nowhere was written the name of Quin Quinlivan, who had crouched in a dark ship's hold, trying to keep the stallion safe during a rough transatlantic journey. Fred Hamilton's name did not appear; nor did that of the late George S. Patton; perhaps most surprising of all, no mention was made of the respected 2nd Cavalry colonel Hank Reed, the right man in the right place at the right time to save this horse's life. A chain of loving hands had passed the horse along virtually since his birth, trying to keep him safe

from the danger that surrounded him. But none of those people who knew him, who cared for him, had been able to hold
on to him. Since the moment of his birth, Witez had belonged
to faceless bureaucracies: the government of Poland, the Third
Reich, the United States Army, and now the Department of
Agriculture.

The ranchers scanned the horse's graceful, swanlike neck
and delicate-featured face. Witez was very much unlike the
compact, muscular American Quarter Horse that was the popular breed in these parts. The ranchers squinted and chewed on
bits of straw; it was hard for Stewart to tell what any of them
was thinking.

As Witez circled the ring, a man in a white cowboy hat sat
high up in the bleachers. This was Earle Hurlbutt, the rancher
who had been pestering for permission to purchase Witez but
was never given the chance—until now. Ever since the stallion
had left Pomona back in November, Hurlbutt had kept his ear
to the ground, hoping to get some news of him. When he heard
about the auction, Hurlbutt hopped in his car and drove from
his barn in Calabasas, California, to Oklahoma, hoping to get
there on time.

For a moment, the horse held everyone in a spellbound
hush. Tom Stewart watched with his heart in his throat. He
knew nothing of the man in the white hat, but he did know that
the 2nd Cavalry's beloved mascot needed to go to a good home.
He said a silent prayer.

Witez had never been sold before, and it was hard to imagine putting a price in dollars on his worth. After a few rounds
of bidding, Earle Hurlbutt knew he had reached his limit. He
made his final bid—eight thousand one hundred dollars—

adjusted the brim of his hat, and then, reluctant to face the disappointment of being outbid, climbed down off the wooden bleachers and walked away.

A man ran up and tapped him on the shoulder, asking where he was going. "You bought yourself a horse," he said.

That May day in 1949 was when Witez finally got his discharge papers and joined civilian life. The "bloody shoulder" coloration on his mother had marked the stallion as a warrior, and for eleven years, as his life was buffeted by armies and war, it had seemed more a curse than a blessing. That spring day in Oklahoma, the curse was broken at last. For the first time in his life, Witez would have a home of his own.

When Tom Stewart realized that the war orphan had found a loving owner, his heart flooded with relief. Here was tangible evidence that his wartime efforts had come to something good. From that day forward, Stewart's heart lightened; the horse he had worked so hard to save had helped to set him free.

32.

THE WIDOW'S ROSE

On October 3, 1950, eight men wearing brown double-breasted jackets and buckskin riding breeches gathered at a New York pier as the *American Importer* docked. Standing a bit apart from the other riders, his lined face lit up with anticipation, was fifty-two-year-old Alois Podhajsky, who had arrived in the city a few days earlier on his first transatlantic flight. The weather was mild and the sky was bright blue. A throng of reporters and photographers clustered to photograph this moment: The famed white Lipizzaner stallions had come to America.

Soon the first stallion appeared on the gangplank, the polished brass of his halter jingling as his hooves thumped on the ramp. He raised his head, flicked his ears, and trumpeted his nostrils, taking in the clanging hubbub of the pier: belching steamships, noisy tugboats, and shouting dockworkers. Picking a familiar face out of the crowd, he lowered his head and let out a warm whinny. At the sight of his beloved Africa, Alois

Podhajsky hurried to the horse's side, whispering a word of greeting, then passing him a sugar lump and kissing him on the nose. Soon all fourteen of the stallions stood in a line, their coats gleaming in the bright afternoon sunshine.

Since moving the horses to Wels in 1946, Podhajsky had painstakingly worked to gain fans for them, taking them to perform in exhibitions around Europe, even giving a demon-stration ride during the London Summer Olympics in 1948. Podhajsky had learned that the graceful magic woven by the white horses could win friends and influence faster than any human could ever hope to. Let them *piaffe, passage,* and pirou-ette. Let them *courbette* and *capriole;* the horses' eloquent silent language turned out to be universal. This was Podhajsky's strat-egy to keep the school alive.

Four weeks after arriving in New York, on November 6, 1950, Alois Podhajsky and his stallions assembled in the cramped schooling area in the basement of Madison Square Garden, their white coats glowing in the dusty air. Africa was missing from the lineup. Podhajsky's favorite had contracted a fever, and tonight he needed to rest. Instead, Podhajsky's second mount, Pluto, would have to do double duty, taking on all of Africa's roles as well as his own. Podhajsky flitted nervously among the horses, giving the grooms instructions for minor adjustments, offering a reminder or two to the riders and a reassuring whis-per to each horse.

A crowd of more than twenty thousand people had gath-ered to watch the show. In the audience, men and women in evening dress chatted softly in expectation of the white stallions' entrance. They excitedly anticipated the show the Spanish Riding School of Vienna would perform.

Podhajsky could feel Pluto's nervous energy as he prepared to enter the large, unfamiliar arena, made spookier (for horses) by the bright lighting that striped the ground with shadows. Podhajsky stroked the stallion on the neck to soothe him, tightened his fingers on the reins, and closed his lower legs around the horse's barrel. This stallion had cowered under a hail of bombs in Vienna under siege; he had accepted reduced rations when food was scarce; he had survived the horror of unsheltered air raids. Through all of that, one man had stayed with him. One man had been there to reassure him, to watch over him, to ride him, and to communicate with him in his own silent language.

As the pair entered the enormous arena, the bright lights made the horse's white coat glow as if lit from within. The babble of twenty thousand people was swiftly replaced by pure silence. Pluto tensed; he flicked a single ear back, intent upon his rider. From the orchestra at ringside came the familiar strains of a Viennese waltz, and the pair broke into a canter.

Despite the strange surroundings, the unfamiliar sounds and sights and smells that greeted them at every turn, Pluto and Podhajsky listened only to each other. The pair seemed to float on the air. At last, they halted in the dead center of the arena, and as the music ended, a collective spellbound hush replaced it—until at last the quiet was broken by a thunderclap of applause. The rest of the program passed in a carefully choreographed blur as stallions and riders perfectly executed their complicated routines. The crowd watched in awe while the white stallions flew into the air or posed as still as statues.

At the end of the program, the announcer came on with a special piece of news: An honored guest had come to watch the horses perform.

Podhajsky and Pluto rode at the head of a single column of horses to the center of the arena. The ring crew rolled out a red carpet. Then a small, elderly woman was escorted down the carpet. Her graying hair was swept up in an elegant coiffure.

The entire arena was plunged into darkness as a single spotlight encircled the two people standing in the arena: Colonel Podhajsky and Beatrice Patton, the general's widow.

In the dark, the crowd was utterly still.

"I am very happy to be able to show you the horses that General Patton, a great American soldier, saved for Austria," Podhajsky said.

"I would give anything if only my husband could be standing here instead of me, for he loved the Lipizzaner so much," Mrs. Patton replied.

As an explosion of photographers' flashbulbs lit up around them, Mrs. Patton handed Podhajsky a single red rose.

33.

THE BIRTHDAY PARTY

Calarabia Ranch, Calabasas, California, January 3, 1965

A radiant blue sky spread over the Calarabia Ranch, and the gates were flung wide open. The beloved King of the Ranch was having a birthday party, featuring a carrot cake and a host of fans from near and far who had come to pay their respects to California's most famous purebred Arabian.

Witez was twenty-seven years old, but his shiny coat, playful manner, and bright eyes were testaments to his excellent health. When Witez arrived in America in 1945, most people had never heard of the Arabian horse. Since then, the breed had gained many fans and was now revered among children for its role in the bestselling Black Stallion series by Walter Farley and the award-winning book *King of the Wind* by Marguerite Henry. All over America, when horse-loving children closed their eyes and imagined an Arabian stallion, they were probably picturing Witez. His portrait was featured in numerous books. Famed illustrator Wesley Dennis painted a well-known portrait of Witez's lost mother, Federajca, with the foal Witez resting at her side in the straw at Janów in Poland. The toy-maker Breyer released a horse statuette modeled on Witez. The Hurlbutts lovingly tended to his fan clubs, answering letters from children and corresponding with people in Europe who remembered him and were happy to know that he had found a peaceful home.

Witez never returned to his birthplace, and this was the cause of much sadness among the Polish people. Their country was one of the hardest hit by the war: It was the location of the most infamous Nazi extermination camps—Auschwitz, Sobibor, Treblinka, and more; it was invaded by both Russia and Germany; and Hitler's murderous plan had been to enslave or murder almost all of its people. Over fifteen percent of Poland's population died during the war. Animals fared little better. Poland's Arabian horse stock—once a point of pride for the country—was mostly lost. After the war ended, its Soviet "liberators" started a second brutal period of totalitarian occupation, which lasted for another forty years.

In spite of these difficulties, Janów Podlaski rebounded once again. And the people of Poland did not forget Witez. His image graced a postage stamp, and many argued that he never should have been sent to America in the first place. There were those who begged for his return—but in the Cold War era, that demand was impossible to meet.

In the end, Witez was like so many others who seemed to have been born in the wrong place at the wrong time. He was a prince with a royal brand on his shoulder, but he was also a refugee. Perhaps that was why he became so beloved. Witez had been hurled into a tragic war for which he bore no responsibility and over which he had no power. Like so many others at that terrible time, he ended up having to start from scratch in a new place, and like so many others, he was lucky to have found kindness and a new home among strangers. Perhaps, like his human counterparts, Witez never forgot his hunger for home, but he thrived in his adopted country.

On his twenty-seventh birthday, as he dined on carrot cake and accepted the love and praise of the gathered well-wishers, Witez still had the regal good looks that had brought him so much fame. His dappled coat shone and his tail floated on the soft California breeze. As he cavorted for his fans in the pastures of Calarabia, the chieftain had never looked more content.

34.

A MIGHTY GOOD AMERICAN

Richmond, Virginia, 1980

On April 7, 1980, thirty-four years to the day after the European horses paraded at Front Royal, Virginia, a message radiated across long-distance phone lines from coast to coast as old army buddies called one another, their voices shaking with the sad news. Hank Reed had been their leader, their mentor, and their father figure. None of the survivors could really believe that he was gone.

Colonel Reed left his regiment on August 12, 1947, to report for duty with Army Ground Forces (later the Army Field Forces) in Fort Monroe, Virginia. In 1948, he was nominated for promotion to brigadier general but chose to retire and take over his family's textile business after his father's death.

Like most men of his generation, Hank Reed did not like to talk about the war. But in his library, along with his books and souvenirs from his days in Germany, a single item rested in the place of honor: his army helmet, nicked and battered in a

silent testimony to its owner's wartime journey across a bleed-
ing continent.

When he returned home from service overseas, Reed found
his two beloved polo ponies, Tea Kettle and Skin Quarter,
healthy and well tended in the pastures of the family farm.
He and his wife, Janice, built a house in the countryside near
Richmond, where they had room for horses. In addition, Reed
had adopted an Arabian mare, Hedschra, and shipped her back
from Germany. After his wartime injury, Reed's hand might
not have been what it used to be, but he rode his horse every
single day.

By the early 1960s, the white stallions whose bloodlines
Reed had helped to save had become world-famous, their every
move followed by adoring fans and the press. They had starred
in a Walt Disney movie called *Miracle of the White Stallions*,
in which Robert Taylor played Alois Podhajsky. If you watch
closely, you might see a scene flash by in which an American
man is eating a bowl of oatmeal while getting a report about
the horses: That unsung hero is Hank Reed. The Disney ver-
sion of the story makes it look as if General Patton were solely
responsible for the rescue of the horses, but the men of the 2nd
Cavalry knew better.

Around the time the movie came out in 1963, Ferdinand
Sperl hosted a 2nd Cavalry reunion in Peoria, Illinois. When
the men asked Reed why he hadn't corrected the record to explain that *he* was responsible for saving the horses at Hostau, he
shrugged and, with the typical modesty of a good soldier, just
said, "Let it be."

While Reed had returned to a quiet private life, Alois

Podhajsky was somewhat of a celebrity, regularly entertaining dignitaries and heads of state. Both Queen Elizabeth II and First Lady Jackie Kennedy had visited the stables in Vienna and watched the horses perform. In 1963, in conjunction with the Disney movie's release, the stallions flew to the United States in resplendent comfort on a transatlantic airline for a whirlwind tour of major American cities. Podhajsky had grown accustomed to long lines of people clamoring to get his autograph. Now, in addition to the horses nibbling up his sugar treats, he seemed to have the whole world eating from his palm.

During that trip to America in 1963, there was an unfinished piece of business for Podhajsky to attend to. On the first night of the horses' grand tour, in Philadelphia, a delegation of officers involved in the horses' rescue walked into the ring. Hank Reed, his face lit by a spotlight, stepped out from the group and strode into the center of the arena. His hair was mostly silver, but nobody could mistake his mile-wide smile.

After nineteen years, Colonel Reed and Alois Podhajsky stood face-to-face in the spotlight. Forgetting all protocol, the two men, overcome with emotion, threw their arms around each other, and thunderous applause rose to the rooftops as the two former soldiers, who had once worn the uniforms of opposing nations, shared a heartfelt embrace.

In 1972, twenty-seven years after the war had ended, Reed and a group of veterans from the 2nd traveled to the American Military Cemetery in Luxembourg. It was Reed's first visit since that long-ago day of Patton's funeral procession. Reed and the other members of the 2nd Cavalry had gone on with their lives in the years since the war, but the faces of the fallen were alive in their memories.

Reed laid a wreath on Patton's grave, then silently stepped away from the other men. Respectfully, the men drew back from their commander, leaving him space to reflect. Apart from the group of veterans, Hank moved from headstone to headstone, laying a single red carnation on the grave of each member of the 2nd Cavalry who was buried there.

The skies over the Hollywood Cemetery in Richmond, Virginia, were a brilliant blue the day Hank Reed was buried. Twenty men from his regiment had come from all over the country to pay their final respects. The lead pallbearer was Jim O'Leary, his faithful driver; over the years, the two had stayed in touch. After the ceremony, Reed's widow told O'Leary that there was something her late husband wanted him to keep: his West Point class ring, worn thin from almost fifty years of use.

Standing around the flag-draped casket as it was lowered into the ground, silver heads bowed and eyes flooded with tears, these veterans gave final salutes. The man being laid to rest had trained them to be soldiers and then led them into battle, never abandoning them, pressing on through tragedy and heartbreak, and eventually leading them to victory. The lives of all the men gathered there were inextricably intertwined with, and all of their lives connected to, their proudest accomplishment: the rescue of the horses.

They remembered Hank Reed as they had first known him: forty-two years old, with crossed cavalry swords pinned on his lapels, and the loose walk and the bighearted gaze of a horse-loving cavalryman. Back in April 1945, he had been an idealist, a dreamer, a believer in far-fetched possibilities. He had listened to the pleas of men who should have been his enemies, and had decided to act. Because of that single moment when he set aside doubt, the horses had been saved.

World War II is still the most destructive event ever to have occurred in human history, with estimates of the total death toll as high as sixty million, or 2.5 percent of the world's total population. The irreparable loss to civilization that resulted from people being slaughtered and entire cultures being obliterated is impossible to measure.

Against the backdrop of all this wreckage, the saving of the horses was a small thing; and yet as Hank Reed's men instinctively knew, it was only through individual acts of compassion that the world was able to climb out of the trough it had dug for itself and attempt to find its way into a more peaceful future.

Later, when people asked why he had decided to save the horses, Colonel Reed's answer was simple: "We were so tired of death and destruction. We wanted to do something beautiful."

35.

THE SPANISH RIDING SCHOOL TODAY

There is a timeless quality to the Spanish Riding School in Vienna. Nowadays, the school resides at the heart of a bustling modern city that still boasts Old World charm. Tourists flock to see the horses perform: The formal performances sell out months in advance. Sunlight filters through the high Palladian windows. Crystal chandeliers, once dismantled piece by piece and hidden away by Alois Podhajsky, hang again in resplendence from the painted ceilings. As the horses practice their timeless movements, the riders continue to share their technique the same way they always have, through word of mouth handed down in an unbroken chain that goes back hundreds of years. That chain of wisdom, based on partnership, love, and kindness, has lasted even longer than any of the political powers that have controlled this institution.

Go to visit the horses in their stables, and for a moment, you might think you're back in the Habsburg Empire. You might expect to see Alois Podhajsky coming around the corner, calling out to each of his beloved stallions by name. Perhaps you will think for just a moment that you have seen Neapolitano Africa or Pluto, looking over their stall doors with lively eyes, ready to whinny a friendly greeting to their friend and master. But no.

Podhajsky, Africa, and Pluto are gone. But their memory lives on. Every time a rider mounts a Lipizzaner, he reflects some of the wisdom that Alois Podhajsky passed along, wisdom that he acquired in more than six decades of working with horses; and each stallion retains some of the genetic makeup passed down through the lines of the original six stallions. Each horse is still named according to his bloodline and wears a brand that denotes his lineage, as has been the custom for hundreds of years. The Spanish Riding School shows a reverence for tradition but has also repeatedly proved that it can reinvent itself. One of the biggest changes since Podhajsky's day is that some of the riders are women.

In the end, it is not only the horses' DNA that determines their ability to perform the brilliant quadrilles and statuesque poses. It is not the gender or race of the riders, nor any precise quality of the bloodstock alone, that allows such extraordinary achievement. In 1945, in a time of war, it was a love of horses that enabled men to rise above their differences and find a way to cooperate. And so it is at the Spanish Riding School today. The discipline embodied in the long, quiet, dignified partnership between man and beast is an act of deep cooperation and silent harmony; it is the very opposite of the Nazi philosophy that once threatened to destroy this beautiful legacy.

EPILOGUE

WHAT BECAME OF THEM?

THE MEN

Colonel Fred L. Hamilton

Fred Hamilton deeply regretted that the demise of the army's remount program occurred during his tenure as head of the Army Remount Service. He was heartbroken that the horses he had brought from Europe, which he had dreamed would have a lasting effect on American horse breeding, mostly failed to live up to their promise in their adopted country. His disappointment is reflected in his labeling of the rescued horses sold off by the Department of Agriculture as "the war orphans." Witez's storybook ending in America was a bright spot in this otherwise mostly unsuccessful attempt to elevate American horse breeding by importing captured European horses.

Wolfgang Kroll

Wolfgang Kroll was known for his tall tales, so the truth of his exploits before and after the war may never be fully known.

After traveling with the horses to America, Kroll returned to Germany, where he got a job working with Lipizzaner horses in the circus. Having managed to secure a letter of recommendation from George Patton himself, he eventually returned to America, where he ended up working at the San Diego Zoo. He then left California and moved to Chicago, where he worked for the Department of Agriculture as an inspector in a meatpacking plant. Along the way, he told people stories about his involvement with the Camel Corps, his days fighting alongside the partisans in Yugoslavia, the hours he spent playing cards with General Patton, and his involvement with the rescue of the Lipizzaners. As incredible as those stories may have seemed, the part about helping to rescue the Lipizzaners was absolutely true.

Rudolf Lessing

The large farm where Rudolf Lessing grew up was situated east of the partition between East and West Germany. After the war, his parents' lands were confiscated and collectivized. His once-affluent family lost everything. Lessing remained with his wife and children in West Germany, continuing to work as a veterinarian. Throughout the rest of his life, he donated his time and knowledge to help rebuild the German horse industry, which had been largely destroyed during the hostilities. After the best of the captured horses were shipped to America, Lessing worked to find homes for the ones from Hostau that had been left behind, in particular the rough-and-ready Russian Kabardins and Panje ponies that the Americans were not interested in importing. Lessing remained friends with the men of the 2nd Cavalry Association, especially Quin Quinlivan, even

Alois Podhajsky instructs his riders at the Spanish Riding School in Vienna.

(left): Gustav Rau explains the fine points of breeding and conformation.

(below): Witez in Germany.

(above): Alois Podhajsky observes a training session at the Spanish Ricing School in Vienna.

(left): Alois Podhajsky guides a Lipizzaner through a *capriole* in hand.

(top): Lipizzaner mares and foals graze peacefully.

(bottom): The Nazi stud farm in Hostau.

Military stud-farm in Hostoun Sumava. Horse Farm Hostoun WWII.

oj. hřebčín v Hostouni na Šumavě. Dvůr Hostouň.

(top): Colonel Hubert Rudofsky driving a four-in-hand in the 1930s.

(middle): Purebreds led by POWs in a Nazi parade.

(bottom): Rudofsky driving a Lipizzaner pair, Poland, 1943.

Lipizzaner horses performing at the Spanish Riding School.

(left): Major Hank Reed riding Tea Kettle, 1942.

(below): Reed leads the newly mechanized 2nd Cavalry.

(top): Rudofsky with Lotnik and another Arabian at Hostau.

(bottom): Captain Ferdinand Sperl with his jeep, nicknamed "Chez Stubby."

(top): Rudolf Lessing riding Indigo.

(bottom): Rudofsky and Reed survey the captured horses in Hostau.

(left): First Lieutenant Tom Stewart in France.

(below): General Patton salutes the Lipizzaner horses during a performance in St. Martin, Austria.

(top): General Patton speaking to Podhajsky at the close of the performance in St. Martin, Austria.

(bottom left): Captain William Quinlivan with Witez at Hostau.

(bottom right): A Lipizzaner being loaded into a crate at Bremerhaven docks.

(top): Witez's foal trots alongside his mother.

(bottom): The horse detectives on the deck of the *Stephen F. Austin* en route to America, October 1945.

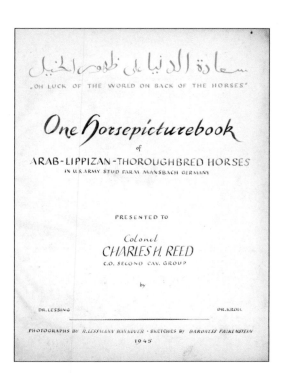

(top): Reed received an album of photos of the rescued horses.

(bottom): Beatrice Patton presents a single rose to Alois Podhajsky at the National Horse Show at Madison Square Garden, 1950.

(top): Witez in fine form at Calarabia Ranch in California.

(bottom): Alois Podhajsky performs for First Lady Jacqueline Kennedy in 1961.

(left): During a Lipizzaner tour of America in 1964, Reed visits with an old friend.

(below): Female riders at the Spanish Riding School.

traveling to America to attend one of their reunions. In 1986, he was recognized at a special performance of the Spanish Riding School and given a medal of honor by the Austrian government.

William Donald "Quin" Quinlivan

Quin Quinlivan, who ran off at the age of seventeen from his home in East Dubuque, Illinois, to join the cavalry, was one of the army's last mounted soldiers. After bidding goodbye to his friend Witez at Front Royal in 1946, he was assigned to the Quartermaster Corps at Fort Robinson, Nebraska, then transferred back to Germany in 1947. On the Europe-bound ship, he met his future wife, Rita McDonald. They were married in Augsburg, Germany, in 1947. In 1949, when Witez was sold at auction, Quinlivan was in Germany, serving as a member of one of the army's last mounted units, fondly known as the Bowlegged Brigade. After he was discharged in 1949, Quinlivan and his wife settled in Los Angeles. He followed the stories about Witez and was delighted by the stallion's growing fame.

Quinlivan never gave up his love for animals. Throughout his life, he adopted unwanted animals—dogs, a bird, even a Shetland pony. Quinlivan saw the Lipizzaners perform once: In 1964, along with Hank Reed, he was part of the 2nd Cavalry delegation invited to Philadelphia to see Podhajsky and the Spanish Riding School. At Quin's funeral in 1985, an Austrian military attaché hand-delivered a floral wreath to honor his contribution to the Lipizzaners and the Spanish Riding School. The Quinlivan family paid more than their fair share to the defense of their nation. Quin's older brother was killed in 1940; his younger brother perished in Korea. Undeterred by their history of sacrifice, Quin's pride in his time in the army no doubt inspired his children, three of whom followed his footsteps into military service. In 1991, his daughter Maureen Nolen, a nurse and army major, was honored during a performance of the Lipizzaner stallions in Nevada.

Gustav Rau

After the war was over, Gustav Rau became one of the most influential horsemen in Germany. He was the first postwar head of the German Olympic Equestrian Committee, and he was revered for discovering the great German horse Halla, the only show jumper ever to win three Olympic gold medals (1956 individual and team, 1960 team). Given credit for rebuilding the German horse industry twice—once after World War I and once after World War II—Rau was honored repeatedly for his contributions to equestrianism in Germany until his death in 1954. The highest equestrian honor in Germany is called the Rau Medal, and in Munich, there is a street named after him, Gustav Rau Strasse, near the Riem Thoroughbred racecourse. But as recent scholarship has uncovered more about Rau's role in the stud farm administration during the Third Reich, his legacy has become more controversial. Some defend him for his part in safeguarding horses during the war, and it is true that the horses within Rau's dominion in general fared better than those in the path of Russian troops. More recently, as German scholars have documented his wartime activities, some have demanded that the street and the prize be renamed due to his activities during the National Socialist period.

Hubert Rudofsky

The last time Hubert Rudofsky ever performed with the Lipizzaners was on Hitler's birthday, in April 1945, in a grand arena
festooned with brilliant scarlet Nazi banners that were wilting
in the rain. By the end of the summer of 1945, the American
GIs billeted in Bohemia had left, and with them, any semblance
of order for the Rudofsky family. The Germans were the hated
oppressors during the war. Now the postwar Czech government made the decision to expel all ethnic German citizens,
even those, like the Rudofskys, whose families had lived in
Bohemia for centuries. All citizens of Bischofteinitz were ordered to leave behind all of their possessions except one suit-
case and were herded into a "resettlement camp" in the Czech
town of Domažlice. Conditions in the camp were difficult, and
Rudofsky's mother died there; her family blamed her death
on medical neglect. Rudofsky avoided the harsh treatment reserved for suspected Nazi collaborators due to his standing in
the community and his official paperwork showing that he had
cooperated with the Americans. All of Lessing's predictions
had come true. Six months after the horses galloped across the
border into Bavaria, everyone involved in the rescue was a free
man except Rudofsky.

The stables at Hostau remained silent, eerie, and empty.
The coaches, the white horses, the busy riders and grooms, all
were like a half-remembered dream that had slipped away. The
rooftops of the stables caved in, and nettles grew up around
the buildings. Nobody remembered that this was a place where
horses once danced. The church in Bischofteinitz where Rudofsky turned heads as he strode down the center aisle in his

cavalry uniform had fallen into decrepitude—many of its treasures had been looted, most of its windows were broken. But
one delicate stained-glass window improbably survived: Its
leaded inscription read "In the war year 1916, the Rudofsky
family offers this window in the hopes that their son will return
safely from the war."

After enduring eighteen months in a resettlement camp,
Rudofsky was released without being charged with any crime.
By that time, his sister had left for America, taking his nephew
and niece with her. He relocated to Germany but never re-
gained his former status in the horse world. Four years after
the war's end, Rudofsky and Lessing ran into each other at an
equestrian event. Rudofsky confided to his friend that his life's
greatest regret was that he had declined Reed's offer to stay
with the Americans. Still, he managed to build a new life for
himself, eventually securing employment at the Donauwörth
stud farm in Bavaria and loaning his expertise to Arabian horse
breeders all over the world. He also amassed an impressive collection of paintings of Arabian horses, most of which are now
housed in the German Museum of the Horse in Verden, Sax-
ony. For a long time, Rudofsky's role in the Lipizzaner rescue
was largely unknown. The Germans' role in securing the horses'
rescue was swept under the rug, and the Spanish Riding School
distanced itself from its wartime association with the German
military. Finally, those wartime animosities started to lessen. In
1986, Rudofsky and Rudolf Lessing were honored at one of
the Spanish Riding School's performances. Six months later,
that performance aired on Austrian TV. That night, perhaps
content that his sacrifice had finally been recognized, Hubert
Rudofsky died in his sleep.

Ulrich (Ulli) Rudofsky

The world that Ulrich Rudofsky had grown up in was all but obliterated by the war. His father, a physician serving on the Eastern Front, spent close to three years as a prisoner of war. He was released but not long after committed suicide, leaving Ulrich's mother alone to manage two young children. After the Americans left Czechoslovakia and her brother-in-law Hubert was imprisoned, Ulli's mother had no choice but to take her two children and flee their home with only a few possessions. She managed to bribe a driver to carry them across the border to Germany. At the border, a Czech guard tried to stop their departure, but an American military policeman intervened and they were allowed to cross, thus escaping internment in the crowded resettlement camp. But the local Germans did not welcome the refugee mother and children back into Germany proper. Their papers were ripped up by a city official, and the boy and his family spent a terrifying month, March 1946, hiding in a stinking cow stable near Schönsee, Germany.

Ulli and his mother and sister eventually emigrated to the United States. After graduating from college, Ulli served in the American army in Germany, patrolling the border but unable to cross the Iron Curtain to the East to see the home he had been forced to leave behind as a ten-year-old. Now a retired pathologist and miniature-shipbuilding enthusiast, he lives near Albany, New York.

Ferdinand Sperl

Swiss-American Ferdinand Sperl, a naturalized citizen of the United States, never lost his enthusiasm for the adopted country he had bravely served. After the war was over, he moved to Peoria, Illinois, where he returned to his first profession of hotelkeeper, taking over as managing director of the Pere Marquette Hotel. Sperl retained his fame in the small town of Kötzting in Germany, where he was remembered for having provided rescued Lipizzaner horses for a traditional local festival just after the German surrender. He returned to Kötzting for the fiftieth anniversary of that celebration, and while there, he was stunned to find that two women in the hotel's restaurant remembered him; when they were schoolgirls, Sperl had come across them as they were fleeing Czechoslovakia on foot with their teachers in April 1945, and he had saved their lives. After this chance meeting, Sperl and the two women remained friends for the rest of his life.

Tom Stewart

Captain Tom Stewart returned to private life after the war. He met his beloved wife, Anne, and together they raised three children. Always humble, he never demanded credit for his daring midnight ride on the favorite horse of King Peter of Yugoslavia in the company of Rudolf Lessing. Throughout the following years, he demurred whenever he was asked to stand in the limelight, especially when it came to his role in rescuing the horses. Finally, in 1996, the modest veteran allowed the Spanish Riding School to honor him for his contributions to preserving the Lipizzaners. During an American tour, he was invited to one of their performances, and in the stables, he was able to visit the descendants of the beautiful animals he had saved. In 2001, he was awarded a National Gold Award by Austria for his wartime role in rescuing the Lipizzaners. One of the longest-lived of the main players in the horse rescue, he passed away in 2006 at the age of ninety-six, more than sixty years after he made that fateful moonlit ride. "The little minister" taught Sunday school at his local church throughout his life.

THE HORSES

Lotnik

Lotnik was auctioned off by the Department of Agriculture in 1948 and purchased by a man who intended to use him as a pleasure horse. When the buyer got divorced, Lotnik was abandoned, eventually being housed in squalid conditions in an ill-kept stable. Fortunately, several years later, the retired former head of the Pomona Remount Depot stumbled across the stallion and recognized him as the pearl of Hostau. Purchased by Bob Aste of the Scottsdale Arabian ranch in 1963, Lotnik lived out the rest of his life on Aste's farm and was a successful sire.

Witez

The chieftain never left his final home at Calarabia except for a brief stay at the ranch of Arabian horse breeder Burr Betts in Colorado from 1960 to 1964. He lived a few months past his twenty-seventh-birthday bash before he died peacefully while sleeping in his pasture. The sign from his days at the Mansbach stud farm that reads "Witez, Field Headquarters" hangs in the International Museum of the Horse in Lexington, Kentucky.

THE PLACES

Fort Riley, Kansas

Once the preeminent horse cavalry locale in America and one of the best in the world, Fort Riley, Kansas, is now home to the 1st Infantry Division, known as "the Big Red One." Horses remained at Fort Riley until 1950, when the last few were led off the base and given refuge for life at the personal ranch of Colonel John Wofford, a member of the 1932 Olympic equestrian team. As these last horses left the hallowed stables at Fort Riley, grown men in uniform, most of them hard-bitten veterans of World War II, lined the streets with tears in their eyes to bid these last chargers, the tail end of a centuries-old tradition, a final farewell. But the spirit of horses remains at Fort Riley. As a fitting tribute to the contribution of horses to the American military, the U.S. Cavalry Memorial Foundation offers individuals the opportunity to memorialize their favorite equine companion with a plaque bearing its name mounted and displayed at the U.S. Cavalry Memorial Research Library located in Fort Riley.

Janów Podlaski

The green-roofed stables of Janów Podlaski are peaceful now, still home to some of the finest Arabians in the world. The town fills up every year for the sale of purebred Arabians that draws horse lovers from around the world. Eighty percent of Poland's Arabians perished between 1938 and 1945, but the stallions Stained Glass and Grand Slam, after fleeing Rau's stud farm in 1944, passed through Dresden during the bombing and were saved by two brave Poles. At the end of the war, the stallions were returned to Poland, forming the nucleus from which the country rebuilt its Arabian breeding program. The stables of Janów Podlaski reopened in the autumn of 1950. Old-timers may still say how much they mourn the loss of their favorite son, Witez, but they probably also know that the stallion was an ambassador for the Polish Arabian and helped increase the breed's renown all over the world.

Hostau/Hostouň

The stud farm at Hostau (now called Hostouň in the Czech language) has been divided up and no longer serves as a horse farm. The mansion where Rudofsky made his home is now a school for delinquent juveniles, and the once-elegant horse stables have fallen into disrepair. Shortly after the war, all ethnic Germans in Czechoslovakia either fled or were forcibly evicted from their homes, leaving behind the majority of their possessions, which were seized by the Czech government and redistributed to its citizens. The ethnic Germans, for complicated reasons that had much to do with history that predated the war, had shown enthusiastic support when Hitler invaded Czechoslovakia in 1938, annexing the Sudetenland as the first step in his brutal war of expansion. The local Czech and Jewish populations suffered greatly under Nazi rule. Because the Germans fought a war of aggression, little sympathy was reserved for their hardship in the aftermath. The loss of the Bohemian Germans' homeland, where their families had lived for centuries, was painful. For many years, due to the closed border between Czechoslovakia and Germany, families who had fled were unable to return to their childhood homes. But with the loosening of restraints after the end of the Soviet era, there has been renewed interest on both sides, Czech and German, in exploring their shared history. There has been increasing interest in the story of the magical Lipizzaners who once lived there, and just a few years ago, a bronze memorial plaque was installed that tells that story in three languages: Czech, German, and English. Citizens in Hostouň dream of restoring the horse farm to its original grandeur and attracting tourists to visit this place where, in the middle of a terrible war, a few men reached past their natural enmity, their different-colored uniforms, and their warring countries to try to do something that was simply good.

AUTHOR'S NOTE

HITLER, HORSE BREEDING, AND THE FLAWED THEORY OF EUGENICS

The story of the brave U.S. soldiers who risked their lives to save Europe's beautiful purebred Lipizzaner and Arabian horses at the end of World War II is thrilling. This courageous rescue showcases qualities we admire: courageousness, selflessness, and cooperation. The facts behind the story—why the world's most violent regime wanted to capture and breed horses—can help us discuss a dark time in human history, when a poorly understood new theory called eugenics was used to fuel prejudice, violence, and murder.

Think about this

Imagine you were sitting in your classroom, and the teacher came in and said that anyone in the class with blue eyes was no longer allowed to go to recess. What if the teacher then said that if your mother had cancer or your father lost his job, you were no longer allowed to attend school? What if you were informed that all children whose parents practiced a certain religion were going to be thrown out of their homes and had to move away?

You would immediately know that these pronouncements were morally wrong. You understand that things like eye color and religion should not form a basis for discrimination, and that when parents have problems, no one should take action against their children. It seems obvious, doesn't it?

So it's difficult to comprehend how many people—educated people with scientific backgrounds—began to believe that discrimination would help improve human society. It all began in a fairly innocent place: on the farm.

What is selective breeding and where did the idea come from?

For many centuries, farmers observed that when breeding plants or animals, it was possible to encourage certain characteristics in offspring, such as size or color, by carefully selecting animals to breed together. The Lipizzaner horse (also known as a Lipizzan), famed for its pure white coat, was not always white. Originally, the horses were many different colors: brown, bay, and chestnut as well as white, but farmers began to keep pedigrees, or records of animals' bloodlines back many generations, and carefully chose only white horses to breed. Eventually, Lippizans became famous for their all-white coats. Today, almost all Lipizzans are born black-brown, brown, or gray but turn white as they age.

Farmers did not focus their attention just on horses. With selective breeding of livestock, farmers were able to produce cows whose milk contained more cream, and dogs that were suited to hunting or guarding sheep or that made good house pets. When animals are bred for the specific needs of humans, they are called domesticated animals. No one protested this activity because these domesticated animals were bred to help humans. In return, humans provided care and feeding for the animals.

In order to breed animals for the particular needs of humans, farmers tended to use observation and trial and error, trying different breeding combinations. It could take many generations before their goals were achieved. In time, farmers also applied these same selective breeding principles to fruits and vegetables, allowing them to develop hardy plants that were resistant to disease.

At first, no one suggested applying these same principles to human beings. The moral codes that governed humans were different from those applied to domesticated animals and crops. Human beings were free to marry whomever they wanted and have children if they wished, and no one had the right to tell them not to. And most importantly, all human beings were considered valuable, whether they were healthy or sick, tall or short.

The new science of genetic inheritance

Though farmers knew it was possible to breed certain characteristics in plants and animals, the science behind it was not well understood. The first person to conduct experiments to better grasp the scientific principles behind selective breeding was a man named Gregor Mendel.

Born in 1822, Mendel was a monk from an area of Europe that is now part of the Czech Republic. Mendel lived in a monastery and he enjoyed working in the garden. He became curious about how pea plants got their specific characteristics. He began to observe the pea plants as they grew, carefully recording details about them, such as their size and the shape and color of their pods, seeds, and flowers. Mendel discovered that when a yellow pea and a green pea were bred, their offspring were always yellow, but in the next generation, some of the peas were green again. Mendel believed that there was a hidden factor contained within the plants that allowed them to pass these traits to their offspring in a manner that could be predicted by science.

Mendel's insights inspired other scientists to figure out exactly how traits were passed along and to take an interest in selective breeding. Researchers began to examine how to breed plants and animals to get desirable characteristics—but this time, using science instead of guesswork.

Charles Darwin and the idea of natural selection

Selective breeding involved domesticated plants and animals—plants grown in gardens and farms, like corn and wheat, and animals raised for help or food, like horses, dogs, cows, and sheep. Around the same time that Mendel was doing his work on domesticated plants, a young English naturalist by the name of Charles Darwin began to observe animals in the wild. Though the two men never met, and developed their theories without hearing of the other's discoveries, their breakthroughs led to the creation of eugenics.

Darwin was fascinated by the bird and animal life in the Galápagos Islands, an isolated chain off the coast of Ecuador. Not only did the islands have an incredible number of species of birds, but each species had a different beak to help it eat a specific kind of food. Why were there so many different kinds of birds, and how did they get their beaks? To explain the variations, Darwin developed a theory he called natural selection.

In Darwin's theory, animals and plants are more likely to live and produce offspring if they have qualities that help them survive. He concluded that over millions of years, tiny changes added up to produce animals with advantageous traits. For example, he theorized, giraffes developed long necks over many generations to gain a competitive edge when they were trying to reach food. Animals with longer necks could reach higher than others, helping them stay alive by reaching the leaves on the tallest trees. Over incredible amounts of time, the only surviving animals were those that had long necks. In natural selection, there was no breeder choosing which traits to emphasize, but only the natural competition for survival in the wild. Traits that helped animals survive were then passed along to their offspring. Later supporters of Darwin's theory, known as Darwinists, called this phenomenon "the survival of the fittest."

Darwin shook the world

Darwin's theory has long been a cornerstone of the life sciences, its accuracy demonstrated over and over again. But at the time, Darwin's ideas were considered radical. He completely changed the way people viewed the world.

One of Darwin's most radical notions was that human development was no different from that of other animals—human beings too had evolved over time. He maintained that many millions of years ago they had developed larger brains and a more upright walking style, which had given them a survival advantage.

The idea of comparing humans to animals shook society. The natural world favored the strong and the resourceful, according to Darwinists. So if human beings took care of the sick and weak, enabling their survival, perhaps our species would become progressively weaker.

After World War I, the huge death toll weighed on people's minds with regard to Darwin's theories. In Europe, between nine and eleven million soldiers had been killed during the war—and soldiers were among the youngest and healthiest citizens. Scientists began to worry that if healthy people died in wars while less healthy people survived, the human race would grow sicker and weaker as a whole. But humans wanted to survive and be strong. If people are no different from animals, some began to say, perhaps we should apply principles that relate to animals to human beings as well. This idea, which was never Darwin's intention, had a terrible outcome when put into practice.

So what was eugenics?

Eugenics was the name given to a scientific theory that became popular in the early part of the twentieth century but was completely discredited by the end of World War II. The idea behind it was that society would be improved if people applied the principles of animal breeding to human populations.

In fact, it was one of Darwin's cousins, an Englishman named Sir Francis Galton, who made up the word "eugenics." This idea, now considered a pseudoscience or fake science, is also called social Darwinism. It holds that the breeding of people should be guided by the same principles farmers used to breed animals. Those who agreed with the theory believed that society would be improved if the weak, sick, or physically or mentally disabled people were not allowed to marry and have children. Some took this a step further, suggesting that "unfit" people should be removed from society.

Events happening at that time made eugenics more attractive. More and more people were moving into cities to work in the factories of the industrial revolution. The fast-growing cities had many problems, such as poverty and disease. Some scientists began to suggest that the problems could be solved with eugenics. They believed that society should eliminate "undesirables," which, to some, included sick people, people who had committed crimes, even orphans who were forced to beg in the streets to stay alive. We now know that this way of thinking was wrong—and led to tragedy.

Hitler, the Third Reich, and the disastrous outcomes of eugenics

Why was eugenics so dangerous? Simply put, because people are not pea plants or white horses. Human beings are complex organisms; even now, more than 150 years after Mendel's discoveries, scientists have an incomplete understanding of human heredity and genes. We know that there are some human traits, such as eye color, that follow simple and predictable patterns, but we also know that more complicated qualities, such as personality, character, and intelligence, are not simple matters of heredity. Even identical twins, who share the exact same heredity, do not necessarily have identical personalities, interests, and values.

Fortunately, the push to improve society by practicing eugenics faded quickly in most places as people realized that there was a fundamental problem with the idea: It was impossible to agree on what made a "good" human being. Some believed that others were inferior because of mental illness or criminal behavior or the color of their skin. Some believed physical disability, choice of religion, or simply being poor was a determining factor. There was some discussion that bad qualities, like laziness, ran in families. So if people believed your father or brother was lazy, then they would believe that you must be lazy too. If that were true and eugenics were in practice, your entire family might be perceived as unfit and could be persecuted and killed or forbidden to have more children. Following practices of eugenics could easily become an excuse for cruelty and discrimination.

Not everyone immediately realized that eugenics was dangerous. The theory took hold in Hitler's Germany and became part of the government's official strategy. In particular, Hitler began to criticize all Jewish citizens, claiming that they were unfit and needed to be removed from Germany. The citizens he preferred were people he called Aryans, who were generally German-speaking, light-skinned Christians. Hitler wanted to remove all the "unfit" people from Germany so that the citizens would be "purebreds." This disastrous decision led to genocide, which means deliberately killing a large group of people for racial, political, or religious reasons.

What happened to eugenics?

When World War II ended, the world became fully aware of the terrible consequences of Hitler's policy of eugenics—about six million Jews died during the Holocaust, most of them starved, enslaved, and deliberately put to death in gas chambers. Hitler masterminded one of the biggest cases of mass murder in human history. Since the end of World War II, most people have understood that human society flourishes when we do not form opinions of people based on their racial or ethnic background, their personal or family characteristics, or their health. Caring for people who are ill makes us stronger, not weaker, and children should not be judged by what their parents look like, how rich they are, or what problems they may have.

The Perfect Horse and eugenics

I was drawn to the story of *The Perfect Horse* because I was inspired by the way that even during wartime, the love of animals could inspire humans to rise above their differences and cooperate. But as I started my research, I realized that I wanted to know not just how the horses were rescued from the secret breeding farm, but why the Nazis had stolen the horses in the first place. As I looked further into history, I realized that Gustav Rau's plan to breed the perfect warhorse was tied to Hitler's evil goal of eliminating all Jews from Germany, something I never would have imagined at the outset. I was shocked to learn that the architects of Hitler's evil plans employing eugenics had also been inspired by horses and that they had used the selective breeding of horses as a blueprint for transforming human society. Do people today understand this history well enough to be sure that we will never repeat it? How can we make sure that the terrible events of Nazi Germany never happen again? In *The Perfect Horse*, we see that Germans, Austrians, Poles, Russians, and Americans set aside their differences to help save the horses. Eugenics and Nazi racial policies instead focused on our differences rather than our common humanity. I hope that anyone who reads *The Perfect Horse* will be reminded that human beings are at our best when we work together. We all must continue to be on guard against the outmoded and dangerous belief that people can be divided and classified like livestock.

A final word

Since the events of *The Perfect Horse* took place, much has changed in the science of animal breeding. We now know that animals develop serious health problems from overbreeding, meaning that people have tried too hard to change the animals' looks or performance through selective breeding. And scientists know that there is much we don't understand about genetic inheritance. We do know, however, that you cannot predict a person's character and performance based on things like their racial or ethnic background, their parents' economic status, or their religion. While the term *eugenics* is no longer in use, the dangerous idea that people can be assigned a value and judged will never entirely go away. Some voices still argue that certain groups of people are undesirable in society. We must continue to fight for justice and equality for all people, and be careful to recognize this flawed way of thinking and protest against it when we see it. While we do inherit some traits from our ancestors, each individual is unique and has equal value to society, and each person deserves equal rights.

ACKNOWLEDGMENTS

To tell a story spanning two continents and more than eight decades is a giant undertaking, and I could not possibly have done it without the help of many people. My greatest debt, without any doubt, is to the families of the veterans who so generously shared their photo albums, old letters, scrapbooks, and personal memories: Reed Johnson; Maureen Quinlivan Nolen; Margaret, Dennis, and Kathleen Quinlivan; Fran Sperl Cooper; Helen Stewart Raleigh; Martha and Virginia Ratliffe; Anne Stewart; Sandi Slisher Konicki; James Hudson Pitman Kelsey; Rick Rudofsky; Kathy O'Leary; and Betty Ann Dunn.

Special thanks to the trustees of the National Sporting Library & Museum in Middleburg, Virginia, who supported me with a John H. Daniels Fellowship in 2010. It was during that time that I first stumbled across a pamphlet describing a parade of Lipizzaner horses in Virginia, which piqued my interest in this fascinating story. Thank you to Bill Cooke, director of the International Museum of the Horse in Lexington, Kentucky, for access to the unparalleled collection of materials about Witez II, and for his great graciousness in helping me with my research. Thanks also to E. Lee Shepard and Jamison Davis at the Virginia Historical Society for their able assistance with the Charles Hancock Reed papers, and to librarians Katherine Staab and Caryn Romo at the W. K. Kellogg Arabian Horse

Library in Pomona, California, for their assistance in locating valuable resources. Thank you to Herwig Radnetter, Karin Nakhai, and the staff of the Spanish Riding School in Vienna for answering so many questions, and for my fascinating visit to the school. Thank you to both Suzanne Christoff at the United States Military Academy Library and Ryan Meyer at the Reed Museum in Vilseck, Germany, for help with historical documents and photographs. Thank you to Esther Buonanno of Tempel Farms for answering questions about the American Lipizzaner and to John H. Daniels Fellow Earl Parker, who graciously shared his research with me. I'm especially indebted to the cheerful and indefatigable Ann Trevor, who sleuthed out a wealth of archival resources for me.

A very special note of gratitude is due to Rick Rudofsky and to Joseph, Isolde, and Reinhold Gruber, who gave me the once-in-a-lifetime experience of touring Germany and the Czech Republic with them as they shared their memories of and reflections on what it was like to live through the events of 1945. Thank you to Balcar Balthazar for sharing Czech perspectives, and to Susi Rudofsky for her vivid recollections of visiting the Lipizzaner horses as a child.

Thank you to Pam Gleason for her expertise about polo and to Robert J. Chambers for his knowledge of carriage driving. Thank you to Victoria Carson for her insights into horse welfare and suggestions for sources. A very special word of thanks to Olympian Jim Wofford, who shared his memories of Fort Riley and his special insights into the men who served in the twentieth-century cavalry.

For help with research, thanks to Nora Alalou for her map-drawing expertise, to Hannah Alalou for assistance with photo research, and to Kimmi Pham and Emily Letts for helping to compile the bibliography. Thank you to Hans Shoeber, Ely Grinwald, Alexandra Lang, Jonathan Larson, and Irene Flotzinger for expert assistance with German-language translation, and to Basia Musik Moltchanov for assistance with Polish pronunciation and translation. Thank you to Iris Busch and her father, Josef Reinhold, for assistance in locating sources from Germany. Many thanks to Daniela Rapp for her ready (and speedy) assistance with German pronunciation.

It takes many people to make a book, and I'm grateful to the outstanding team at Ballantine for all of their work. I am deeply indebted to my brilliant editor, Susanna Porter, whose patience, meticulousness, and gift for narrative structure helped me chisel out this story from the giant rock of information. A special note of thanks goes to Priyanka Krishnan, whose insightful reading of the first draft helped so much to hone the structure of the story. Thanks to Kim Hovey, Steve Messina, Rachel Kind, Robbin Schiff, and Cheryl Kelly, who have gone above and beyond for me so many times.

Great thanks as well to my agent, Jeff Kleinman of Folio Literary Management, whose enthusiasm, kindness, and quick mind make my writing life and my stories better in so many ways.

Much love to my writer buddies who make it all bearable: Lauren Baratz-Logsted, Jon Clinch, Renee Rosen, Danielle Younge-Ullman, Jessica Keener, Karen Dionne, Melanie Benjamin, and Darcie Chan; to Andrew Grant for his special insight into wartime animal stories; and to the brilliant Tasha Alexander, who will read a draft at any time of day or night and always says the right thing.

Love and gratitude to my mother, Virginia Letts, who listened as I read each draft out loud, and whose comments, while sparing, were always insightful. And as always to my patient and wonderful family, Ali, Joseph, Nora, Hannah, and Willis, who rarely complain about burnt dinners, and never suggest that I get a real job.

A special word of appreciation to Marguerite Henry, whose book *White Stallions of Lipizza* inspired my lifelong fascination with the Spanish Riding School. And most of all a heartfelt thank-you to all of the wonderful men, women, and children who love horses and have written me letters, called me, invited me to speak or visit book clubs, and engaged in wonderful conversations on social media. Above all, it was your passion for great equestrian stories that encouraged me to tackle the story of the white stallions.

BIBLIOGRAPHY

INTERVIEWS AND PERSONAL CORRESPONDENCE WITH AUTHOR

Robert J. Chambers (RJC)
Fran Sperl Cooper (FS)
Bryan Dickerson (BD)
John S. Dolibois (JD)
Elizabeth Ann Dunn (EAD)
Pam Gleason (PG)
Reed Johnson (RJ)
Sandra Slisher Kanicki (SSK)
James Hudson Pitman Kelsey (JK)
Jan Maiberg (JM)
Maureen Quinlivan Nolen (MQN)
Kathy O'Leary (KO)
Dennis Quinlivan (DQ)
Margaret Quinlivan (MQ)
Herwig Radnetter (HR)
Ulrich Rudofsky (UR)
Anne Stewart (AS)
James Wofford III (JW)

FAMILY PAPERS

Fran Sperl Cooper (FS papers)
Reed Johnson (RJ papers)
Sandra Slisher Kanicki (SSK papers)

James Hudson Pitman Kelsey (JHPK papers)
Kathy O'Leary (KO papers)
Quinlivan Family (QF papers)
Ulrich Rudofsky (UR papers)
Stewart Family (SF papers)

ARCHIVAL COLLECTIONS

The International Museum of the Horse, Arabian Horse
    Collection (IMH)
Kellogg Arabian Library (KAL)
National Archives and Research Administration (NARA)
National Sporting Library (NAS)
Reed Museum
United States Military Academy
Virginia Historical Association (VMA)

WORKS CONSULTED

"255,700 Men in U.S. Army; Only 2,954 Are Colored." *Baltimore Afro-
American*, December 15, 1934.
"2d Cavalry Regiment." *The Dragoon* I (July/August 2012).
"8-Year-Old German Stallion Brings Top Price at Auction." Undated
clipping (IHA).
Agriculture Remount Service Catalogue of Horses to Be Sold at Public Auction.
Fort Reno, Oklahoma, 1949 (NAS).
Allen, David. "Pomona's K Is for a Man Who Was Truly Grrreat!" *Inland
Valley Daily Bulletin*, September 25, 2004.
Allen, Robert S. "Patton Visioned as Unit of Cavalry." *The Salt Lake
Tribune*, 1946, 4.
"American Gets 'Emperor's Horse.'" *The New York Times*, December 13,
1945.
"Arabian Horse Breeding Farm to Change Hands." *Los Angeles Times*, 1947.
"Arabian Horse Display Draws Many Tourists." *The Washington Post*, 1942.

"Arabian Horses Given to War Department: Club Act to Help Defense and Preserve the Strain." *The New York Times*, October 19, 1941.

"Arabian Horses Given to War Department." *The New York Times*, 1941.

"Arco-Valley Held as Foe of Hitler." *The New York Times*, 1933.

"Arms Before Men." *Time*, August 22, 1938.

"Army and Rambler Polo Fours Victors." *The New York Times*, 1922.

"Army Team Fete Visiting Polo Players: Participants Are Guests at Dinner in Army-Navy Club." *The Washington Post*, June 11, 1936.

"Army to Get Lipizzaner Stallion." *The New York Times*, 1964.

"Army to Increase Its Horse Cavalry." *The New York Times*, 1940.

"Army to Use Arabian Stud Farm." *The New York Times*, 1943.

Arnold, Dietbert. *Gespräche mit einem Pferdemann* (Bremen: Pferdesport-Verlag Ehlers, Gmbh, 1995).

"Athletes Spurred by Reich Officials." *The New York Times*, 1935.

"Austria." United States Holocaust Memorial Museum, www.ushmm.org.

"Average American No Adonis to Science." *The New York Times*, August 22, 1932.

Bartlett, Arthur. "The War Horse Comes Back: Military Experts Said the Cavalry Was Dead." *The Sun*, 1941.

"The Battles of Lunéville: September 1944." *Military History Online*, www .militaryhistoryonline.com.

Betts, Burr. "Witez II." *The Arabian Horse Journal*, July 1977.

"Big Maneuvers Test US Army." *Life*, October 6, 1941.

Black, Edwin. *War Against the Weak: Eugenics and America's Campaign to Create a Master Race* (New York: Four Walls Eight Windows, 2003).

Blumenson, Martin. *The Patton Papers* (Boston: Houghton Mifflin, 1972).

Boker, John R., Jr. "Report of Initial Contacts with General Gehlen's Organization." *Forging an Intelligence Partnership: CIA and the Origins of the BND, 1945–1949* (CIA History Staff, Center for the Study of Intelligence, European Division, 1999).

Brandts, Ehrenfried. *Pferde zwischen den Fronten: Polnische Staatsgestüte und das Schicksal des Hengstgestüts Drogomysl/Draschendorf unter deutscher Besatzung 1939–1945* (Munich: Zugvogel Verlag Wenzel, 2007).

"Brilliant Setting for Society Circus." *The Washington Post*, 1922.

Brown, Gordon. "Meet Vast, Army Wonder Horse Which Can Gallop Backward." *The Washington Post*, 1940.

Case, Carole. *The Right Blood: America's Aristocrats in Thoroughbred Racing* (New Brunswick, NJ: Rutgers University Press, 2001).

Catalogue of Thoroughbreds, Property of the U.S. Remount Service to Be Sold by Public Auction at Aleshire Quarter Master Depot (Remount), Front Royal, Virginia. Pamphlet, 1946 (NSP).

Chavez, Stephanie. "Horse Lovers Head for the Shrine." *Los Angeles Times*, 2001.

Clark, Alfred E. "Charles H. Reed, 79, the Colonel Who Rescued Lipizanner Horses." *The New York Times*, 1980.

Clay, Steven E. "US Army Order of Battle 1919–1941." *Combat Studies Institute Press* II (2010).

"Clinical History of Crime." *The New York Times*, 1925.

"Cole Heads Army Riders." *The New York Times*, 1938.

Cole, Hugh M. *European, Mediterranean, Middle East Theaters of Operations* (Washington, D.C.: United States Army Center of Military History, 2002).

"Commissions Given 132 at West Point." *The New York Times*, 1922.

Corrigan, Joseph E. "They Say." *The New York Times*, 1930.

Cullum, George W. *Biographical Register of the Officers and Graduates of the U.S. Military Academy*, Vol. VII (Chicago: R. R. Donnelley & Sons Company, 1931).

Daley, Arthur J. "Largest U.S. Team in History, 395, Will Compete in Olympic Games." *The New York Times*, 1936.

Daniell, Raymond. "Pity for Germans Grows in U.S. Ranks." *The New York Times*, 1945.

Daume, Anja. *Galoppieren gegen den Wind: Gestütsgeschichte Mansbach: Vision & Wirklichkeit* (Norderstedt, Germany: Books on Demand, 2009).

Davis, Susan. "Operation Cowboy." *Sports Illustrated*, October 16, 1995.

De Amicis, Albert. *General George S. Patton, Jr., and the U.S. 2nd Cavalry (Patton's Ghosts of the Third Army)*, University of Pittsburgh's Graduate School of Public and International Affairs, July 17, 2008.

D'Este, Carlo. *Patton: A Genius for War* (New York: HarperCollins, 1995).

"Die Lipizzaner und der Kötztinger Pfingstritt 1945," *601 Jahre Kötztinger Pfingstritt*. Author's personal collection.

DiMarco, Louis A. "The Army Equestrian Olympic Team." Louis DiMarco home page, www.louisdimarco.com.

———. *War Horse: A History of the Military Horse and Rider* (Yardley, UK: Westholme Publishing, 2008).

Dolibois, John. *Pattern of Circles: An Ambassador's Story* (Kent, OH: Kent State University Press, 1989).

———. Interview with John Dolibois, May 11, 2000, RG-50.030*0408, United States Holocaust Memorial Museum, collections.ushmm.org.

Douglas, R. M. *Orderly and Humane: The Expulsion of the Germans After the Second World War* (New Haven, CT: Yale University Press, 2012).

"Dressage Experts." *The New Yorker*, November 5, 1950.

"Drew Pearson on the Washington Merry-Go-Round." News Release, Bell Syndicate, November/December 1945.

Dyer, George. *XII Corps Spearhead of Patton's Third Army*. Report, 1945.

"Eugenics Conference Opens Here Today." *The New York Times*, August 13, 1932.

"Europe Is Offering an Extensive List of Fall Attractions." *The Christian Science Monitor*, 1938.

"European Horses Captured by Army Pose Problem." *The Christian Science Monitor*, December 3, 1947.

Evans, Richard J. *The Third Reich at War* (New York: Penguin Press, 2009).

"Even Atom Age Can't Displace War Horse. Animals Still Needed, Retired Officer Says." *Chicago Daily Tribune*, February 23, 1948.

"Eyewitness Gotz Bergander Recalls the Bombing of Dresden." *German History in Documents and Images*, Nazi Germany 1933–1945, ghi-dc.org.

Fahnenbruck, Nele Maya. ". . . *Reitet für Deutschland*": *Pferdesport und Politik im Nationalsozialismus* (Göttingen, Germany: Die Werkstatt, 2013).

Foster, Renita. "American Cowboys Ride to the Rescue." *Armor*, 1998, 22–23.

Frederic, Sondern. "The Wonderful White Stallions of Vienna." *Reader's Digest*, April 1963.

Freilinghaus, Eckkehard. "Hubert Rudofsky." *Arabische Pferde*, 151.

———. "Hubert Rudofsky ein Grandseigneur der Welt des Pferdes." *Trankhener Hefte*, undated, from Rudofsky family papers. "Ft. Myer Society Circus Is Success; Two Shows Today." *The Washington Post*, 1933.

"Gen. Patton Helped Save Famed White Stallions." *The Washington Post*, 1966.

"German Army Jumpers Win the Lion's Share of Horse Show Honors." *Brooklyn Daily Eagle*, December 13, 1930.

"German Horse Wins at Garden." *The Washington Post*, 1946.

"German Visitors Learn Their ABCs of Trotting at Goshen." *Middletown Times Herald*, 1938.

Godfrey, A. H. "Driving Four-in-Hand." *Outing*, May 1897, 107–12.

Golden, Chris, ed. "History, Customs and Traditions of the 'Second Dragons,' the Oldest Continuously Serving Mounted Regiment in the United States Army." In *2d Cavalry Association* (Newton, MA: 2d Cavalry Association, 2011), 1–56.

"Gustav Rau Led Olympic Riding Team." *The New York Times*, December 6, 1954.

Hanlin, J. J. "The General and the Horses." *The American Legion Magazine*, 1963, 22–43.

The Heimatbrief: A Newsletter Magazine of the German Bohemian Heritage Society 17 (March 2007) and 19 (September 2008).

"Here for the National Horse Show." *The New York Times*, October 3, 1950.

Herr, John K. *The Story of the U.S. Cavalry 1776–1942* (Boston: Little, Brown, 1956).

Higgins, Alice. "From the Near East to the Far West." *Sports Illustrated*, March 11, 1963.

Hitler, Adolf, trans. Ralph Manheim. *Mein Kampf* (Boston: Houghton Mifflin, 1943).

"Hitler Watches Equestrians Win Show." *The New York Times*, February 10, 1934.

Hofmann, George F. *Through Mobility We Conquer: The Mechanization of U.S. Cavalry* (Lexington: University Press of Kentucky, 2006).

Holt, Carlyle. "America Builds an Army. Cavalry Horse Just Like His Rider Gets 13 Weeks of Basic Training." *The Boston Daily Globe*, January 9, 1943.

Holz, Louis T., ed. "Thoroughbred: Second Cavalry Association." *Newsletter #59*, Summer 1980.

"Horse Show Ball Is Set for Nov. 3." *The New York Times*, 1950.

"Horses Arriving from Europe for the Garden Show." *The New York Times*, October 1, 1950.

"Horses Held Booty." *Chicago Daily Tribune*, January 14, 1948.

Hughes, Allen. "Lipizzaner at the Garden." *The New York Times*, 1964.

Iggers, Wilma, and Georg Iggers. *Two Lives in Uncertain Times: Facing the Challenges of the 20th Century as Scholars and Citizens* (New York: Berghahn Books, 2006).

"Imported Horses Attract Throng at Front Royal." *The Washington Post*, 1946.

Isenbart, Hans-Heinrich, Emil M. Bührer, and Kurt Albrecht. *The Imperial Horse: The Saga of the Lipizzaners* (New York: Knopf, 1986).

"James H. Pitman 1940 Cullum Number 2006, September 18, 1944. Died in Lunéville, France." www.westpoint.edu.

Keane, Michael. *Patton: Blood, Guts, and Prayer* (New York: Regnery, 2012).

"Kellogg Arabian Horse Farm Turned Over to Army." *Los Angeles Times*, November 2, 1943.

"Kellogg Farm Fate in Brannan Hands." *Los Angeles Times*, December 2, 1948.

Kershaw, Ian. *The End: The Defiance and Destruction of Hitler's Germany, 1944–1945* (New York: Penguin Press, 2011).

Kevles, Daniel J. *In the Name of Eugenics: Genetics and the Uses of Human Heredity* (New York: Knopf, 1985).

Keyser, Tom. "Aging GI Reflects on WWII Rescue of Lipizzaner Stallions." *Laredo Morning Times*, 2005.

"King of the Wing Review." *The New York Times*, November 14, 1948.

Knapp, George. "Buffalo Soldiers at Fort Leavenworth in the 1930s and Early 1940s: Interviews Conducted by George Knapp." Combat Studies Institute, U.S. Army Command and General Staff College, April 1991.

Kochanski, Halik. *The Eagle Unbowed* (New York: Penguin, 2013).

Kowalczyk, Andra. *Tennessee's Arabian Horse Racing Heritage* (Charleston, SC: Arcadia, 2007).

Kugler, Georg, and Paula Boomsliter. *The Lipizzan Horse: A Guide to Vienna's Spanish Riding School and Lipizzaner Museum* (Florence, Italy: Bonechi, 2002).

Lambert, A. L., and G. B. Layton. *The Ghosts of Patton's Third Army: A History of the Second U.S. Cavalry.* Compiled, edited, and published by Historical Section, 2nd Cavalry Association, 1946.

Leerhsen, Charles. *Crazy Good: The True Story of Dan Patch, the Most Famous Horse in America* (New York: Simon & Schuster, 2008).

Legendary White Stallions, DVD. Directed by Michael Schlamberger. PBS, 2013.

"Letter." Charles Hancock Reed to Mrs. O'Leary, September 29, 1945 (KO papers).

Livingston, Phil, and Ed Roberts. *War Horse: Mounting the Cavalry with America's Finest Horses* (Albany, TX: Bright Sky Press, 2003).

Loch, Sylvia. *The Royal Horse of Europe: The Story of the Andalusian and Lusitano* (London: J. A. Allen, 1986).

"Los Angeles Briefs." *Los Angeles Times*, May 5, 1946.

Ludwig, Dieter. "Inge Theodorescu—eine große Pferdefrau lebt nicht mehr," ludwigs-pferdewelten.de, April 12, 2010.

Luft, Monika. "The Lots of Arabian Horses in Poland, Part 1: The World War I and the Bolshevik Invasion." *Arabians Horse Mag.* www.polskiearaby.com, March 21, 2011.

———. "The Lots of Arabian Horses in Poland, Part 2: World War II." *Arabians Horse Mag.* www.polskiearaby.com, April 6, 2011.

MacCormac, John. "Austria Will Send Famed Horse Unit." *The New York Times*, 1950.

MacDonogh, Giles. *After the Reich: The Brutal History of the Allied Occupation* (New York: Basic Books, 2007).

Malone, Michael. "Stolen by the Nazis: The Tragic Tale of 12,000 Blue-Eyed Blond Children Taken by the SS to Create an Aryan Super Race." *Daily Mail* (London), January 9, 2009.

"The Man Originating from the Sudentenland Found a New Home in Boxberg." Undated clipping (UR papers).

Martin, Frank Wayne, and Nancy Martin. *Patton's Lucky Scout: The Adventures of a Forward Observer for General Patton and the Third Army in Europe* (Milwaukee: Crickhollow Books, 2009).

McGuire, Phillip. *Taps for a Jim Crow Army: Letters from Black Soldiers in World War II* (Santa Barbara, CA: ABC-Clio, 1983).

McLaughlin, Kathleen. "Patton Gives Up Army to Truscott." *The New York Times*, 1945.

Michael, John. *Fort Myer* (Charleston, SC: Arcadia, 2011).

Morgan, M. H. *The Art of Horsemanship by Xenophon* (London, 1894).

"Mrs. Patton's Fall Is Fatal." *The Sun*, October 1, 1953.

"Name Adolf Held Banned for German Police Horses." *The New York Times*, 1943.

NASS News: The Official Newsletter of the North American Shagya-Arabian Society, September 2008, 1–14.

"National Defense: Horses on Wheels." *Time*, August 19, 1940.

"The Nazi Olympics Berlin 1936." United States Holocaust Memorial Museum, August 18, 2015.

"New Problem for Senate: 234 Horses." *The Washington Post*, December 2, 1947.

"New Removals Slash Kellogg Ranch Herd." *Los Angeles Times*, 1948.

"Now Men on Horseback Team Up with Machines." *Life*, April 21, 1941, 86–93.

"Ocean Travelers." *The New York Times*, 1938.

"Official Denies Horses Booty." *The Washington Post*, December 12, 1947.

"Operation Cowboy: The Saving [*sic*] the Lipizzaner Horses by Troop A, 42nd Squadron Mecz 2nd Cavalry Group (The Ghosts of Patton's Third Army)," www.gjt.cz.

O'Shaughnessy, Edward J., Jr. *The Evolution of the Armored Force, 1920–1940* (United States Army War College, 1993).

"Our Hitler (1945)." German Propaganda Archive, www.calvin.edu.

Parker, Earl. "The Remount Service and Its Stallions: Rescue of the WWII Hostau POWs and of the Lipizzans, Part I." *Haute École* 20, no. 4 (Summer 2012).

Path to Glory: The Rise and Rise of the Polish Arabian Horse. Directed by Jen Miller and Sophie Pegrum. Horsefly Films, 2011.

"Patterson Arabians." *Arabian Horse World*, June 1977.

Pawelec-Zawadska, Izabella, "Andrzej Krzyształowicz." *Magazyn z M do M*, January 1998.

Peter, Brigitte. "Hostau 1945: Die Rettung der Lipizzaner—Wagnis oder Wunder? Die Rettung der weissen Pferde am Ende des II. Weltkrieges." *Zyklus* 2–4 (1982).

Piekałkiewicz, Janusz. *The Cavalry of World War II* (New York: Stein and Day, 1980).

Podhajsky, Alois. *The Complete Training of Horse and Rider in the Principles of Classical Horsemanship* (Garden City, NY: Doubleday, 1967).

———. *My Dancing White Horses* (New York: Holt, Rinehart and Winston, 1965).

———. *My Horses, My Teachers* (North Pomfret, VT: Trafalgar Square Publishing, 1997).

Powell, Horace B. *The Original Has This Signature: W. K. Kellogg* (Battle Creek, MI: W. K. Kellogg Foundation, 1989).

"Prize Horses Seized in Hungary to Be Sold." *The Washington Post*, November 21, 1947.

"Question of Ownership of Captured Horses: Hearings before a Subcommittee of the United States Senate. Eightieth Congress. First Session. December 3–23, 1947." United States Government Printing Office, 1947.

Ragan, Jean. "A Horse and His Friend." *The Denver Post*, April 30, 1961.

Rau, Gustav. *Die Reitkunst der Welt an den olympischen Spielen 1936. L'Art équestre du monde . . . International Equitation, Etc.* (Hildesheim, Germany: Olms Presse, 1978).

"Reich Equestrians Arrive for Shows. German Party to Visit Sport's

Centers. Group Attends Races at Belmont." *The New York Times*, May 10, 1938.

Rendel, John. "10,000 See Horse Show Opening; Mexican Girl Wins Feature Jump." *The New York Times*, 1950.

Robinson, Ruth. "Lipizzaner Stallions, Due May 19, Attract Big Benefit Parties." *The New York Times*, 1964.

Robson, Seth. "Czech Republic Pays Tribute to WWII Heroes. Memorial to Honor Soldiers Who Saved Lipizzaners, POWs." *Stars and Stripes*, April 9, 2006.

"Rommel's Arabian Horse in Windsor Castle Stable." *The New York Times*, 1946.

Rosmus, Anna. *Czech Incursions: Foreign Horses Going Home* (Anna Elisabeth Rosmus, 2014).

"Royal Horses Will Be Sold." *The Washington Post*, November 20, 1947.

Schoomaker, Eric B., and Russell J. Czerw. *The United States Army Medical Department Journal*, 2009.

"Scientists Display Heredity Control." *The New York Times*, 1929.

Shirer, William L. *The Rise and Fall of the Third Reich: A History of Nazi Germany* (New York: Simon & Schuster, 1960).

Smith, Krista. "Historic Sagamore Farm: New and Improved." *Baltimore Fishbowl*, May 17, 2013.

Smith, Linell Nash. *And Miles to Go: The Biography of a Great Arabian Horse, Witez II* (Boston: Little, Brown, 1967).

"Society Circus at Fort Myer Begins Friday." *The Washington Post*, 1932.

"Stallion Brings $20,300; Young Pawley Gets German-Bred Nordlicht at Auction." Undated clipping (IMA).

Steen, Andrew K. "W. R. Brown's Maynesboro Stud." *Modern Arabian Horse*, September 12, 2012, 44–51.

Sternthal, Barbara. *The Lipizzans and the Spanish Riding School Myth and Truth* (Vienna: Brandstätter, 2010).

"Sysonby's Body Exhumed." *The New York Times*, 1906.

Tavel, Emilie. "Hungary Asks U.S. to Return Thoroughbred Horses." *The Christian Science Monitor*, December 4, 1947.

Tedesco, Vincent J., III. "'Greasy Automations' and 'The Horsey Set':
The U.S. Cavalry and Mechanization, 1928–1940." Master's thesis,
Pennsylvania State University, 1995.

"The Thoroughbreds from Germany. Not a Shadow of a Doubt." *The
Blood-Horse*, November 9, 1946.

Thurtle, Phillip. "Harnessing Heredity in Gilded Age America: Middle
Class Mores and Industrial Breeding in a Cultural Context." *Journal of
the History of Biology*, 2002, 43–78.

Totten, Ruth Ellen Patton, and James Patton Totten. *The Button Box:
A Daughter's Loving Memoir of Mrs. George S. Patton* (Columbia:
University of Missouri Press, 2005).

Trimborn, Harry. "Polish Breeders of Prize Arabian Horses Fear National
Turmoil's Impact." *Los Angeles Times*, 1982.

Truscott, Lucian K., Jr. *The Twilight of the U.S. Cavalry: Life in the Old
Army, 1917–1942* (Lawrence: University Press of Kansas, 1989).

"Um die 50. Lipizzaner sollen dabei gewesen sein." *601 Jahre Kötztinger
Pfingstritt*. Author's personal collection.

"Use Army Horses in Polo." *The New York Times*, 1922.

Waller, Anna. *Horses and Mules in the National Defense* (Washington,
D.C.: U.S. Army Quartermaster Corps, 1958).

"'War Booty' Horses Viewed by 8 Officials." *The Washington Post*,
December 7, 1947.

Westerman, Frank. *Brother Mendel's Perfect Horse: Man and Beast in an
Age of Human Warfare* (London: Vintage Digital, 2012).

Wiener, Tom. *Forever a Soldier: Unforgettable Stories of Wartime Service*
(Washington, D.C.: National Geographic Society, 2005).

Wilson, Paul. *Himmler's Cavalry: The Equestrian SS, 1930–1945* (Atglen,
PA: Schiffer, 2000).

"The W. K. Kellogg Arabian Horse Ranch." *Los Angeles Times*, January 2,
1931.

The XIth Olympic Games, Berlin, 1936: Official Report (Berlin: Wilhelm
Limpert, 1937).

Zaloga, Steve, and Tony Bryan. *Lorraine 1944: Patton vs. Manteuffel*
(Oxford, UK: Osprey Military, 2000).

IMAGE CREDITS

Page 13: courtesy of Reed Johnson (*top*); courtesy of the Quinlivan family (*bottom*)

Page 14: courtesy of Reed Johnson (*top*); Associated Press (*bottom*)

Page 15: courtesy of the International Museum of the Horse, Lexington, Kentucky (*top*); Associated Press (*bottom*)

Page 16: courtesy of the Virginia Historical Society (*top*); Leonhard Foeger/Reuters Pictures (*bottom*)

INDEX